Transnational Filipina/o/x Youth, Intersectional Identities, and School-Community Partnerships

This book provides an in-depth examination of how Filipina mothers, serving as migrant caregivers, and their children navigate the experiences of family separation and reunification through Canada's Live-in/Caregiver Program (L/CP).

It analyses how Filipina/o/x youth understand their political agency, the legacy of colonialism, and their sense of identity and belonging in urban schools through school-community partnerships. The work examines the global migration experiences of transnational Filipina/o/x youth and their mothers in nation-states such as Canada through the lens of the global domestic work industry. It connects the theoretical frameworks of critical and intersectional feminisms within a transnational context to the specificity of settler colonialism within Canada, a white settler nation-state. It underscores the pivotal role of school-community partnerships in facilitating the political agency of Filipina mothers and their children, and in shaping Filipina/o/x youths' transnational identities through equitable educational policies and, ultimately, im/migration policies and practices. This book is a valuable addition to the discourse on global migration, transnational feminism, and critical race studies in education.

The book primarily targets scholars, researchers, graduate students in the fields of Gender Studies, Education, Psychology, Mental Health, Immigration/Transnational Studies, and Asian Canadian Studies. It is particularly relevant for those with specialist knowledge in Gender and Immigration Studies, as well as Equity and Social Justice Education, which includes a focus on supporting the participation of racialized im/migrants in the school system.

Jessica Ticar is a Canadian Certified Counsellor with the Canadian Counselling & Psychotherapy Association and an interdisciplinary scholar. She received her PhD from Western University, Canada and is an Assistant Professor at the School of Social Work, Algoma University (Brampton Campus).

Routledge Critical Studies in Gender and Sexuality in Education

Series Editors Wayne Martino, EJ Renold, Goli Rezai-Rashti, Jessica Ringrose and Nelson Rodriguez

29 Affect and the Making of the Schoolgirl
A New Materialist Perspective on Gender Inequity in Schools
Melissa Joy Wolfe

30 Rethinking School Spaces for Transgender, Non-binary and Gender Diverse Youth
Trans-ing the School Washroom
Jennifer Ingrey

31 Facilitating LGBTQIA+ Allyship through Multimodal Writing in the Elementary Classroom
Preparing Teachers to Challenge Heteronormativity
By Judith M. Dunkerly, Julia Poplin, and Valerie Sledd Taylor

32 Gendered and Sexual Norms in Global South Early Childhood Education
Understanding Normative Discourses in Post-Colonial Contexts
Edited by Deevia Bhana, Yuwei Xu, and Vina Adriany

33 LGBTQI+ Allies in Education, Advocacy, Activism, and Participatory Collaborative Research
By Wendy M. Cumming-Potvin

34 Towards a Queer and Trans Ethic of Care in Education
Beyond the Limitations of White, Cisheteropatriarchal, Colonial Care
By Bishop Owis

35 All About Black Girl Love in Education
bell hooks and Pedagogies of Love
Edited by Autumn Griffin and Yolanda Sealey-Ruiz

Transnational Filipina/o/x Youth, Intersectional Identities, and School-Community Partnerships

The Gendered Vulnerabilities of Migration in Canada

Jessica Ticar

NEW YORK AND LONDON

First published 2025
by Routledge
605 Third Avenue, New York, NY 10158

and by Routledge
4 Park Square, Milton Park, Abingdon, Oxon, OX14 4RN

Routledge is an imprint of the Taylor & Francis Group, an informa business

ISBN: 978-1-032-26270-3 (hbk)
ISBN: 978-1-032-26271-0 (pbk)
ISBN: 978-1-003-28746-9 (ebk)

DOI: 10.4324/9781003287469

Typeset in Times New Roman
by KnowledgeWorks Global Ltd.

Contents

1 Introduction

Mobilizing the impact of Canada's Live-in/Caregiver Program through political agency

> I learned…the meaning of family…the meaning of having questions.
>
> (Bryan, 18 years old)

Introduction

Uninformed about his mother's decision to leave the Philippines and migrate within Canada's Live-in/Caregiver Program(s) or L/CP[1], Bryan understood the parameters of his mother's decision to leave, "she did this for us", meaning for their family, upon reflection as an 18-year-old, while simultaneously recalling a memory of feeling abandoned:

> She left while we were sleeping or she would think I was sleeping…So I opened my eyes and saw her crying. And I didn't want to say anything because I thought I was in trouble so then she left, and I thought it was a dream so I slept again, but when I woke up, mom was gone, but it didn't really affect me too much because I thought she was just gonna come back… But, like after a year passed, I found out that she wasn't coming back, and I just kept it to myself. I never asked where she was. I never cried when she left because a part of me knew that she was doing it for us. I learned parenting from a very young age. I learned how to be responsible, how to live with myself, how to do jobs, simple stuff, but like, the meaning of family, the meaning of having questions, like, why did my mom leave me?
>
> (Bryan, 18 years old)

This book explores these particular questions that Bryan proposes, examining how he has "reinvented [himself] as new [subject]" (Roces, 2021, p. 8) through political agency. His feelings of maternal abandonment are juxtaposed with the life skills and epistemological understandings of 'family' gained through mobilizing the traumas of separation and reunification of Canada's L/CP. Bryan's sentiment, "why did my mom leave me?" was shared with many of Filipina/o/x[2]

DOI: 10.4324/9781003287469-1

youth in this book, where these embodied words reverberated like ghosts of the past, haunting Filipina/o/x youth as they shared their stories of separating from their mothers in the present. Their mothers "leaving" them had a significant impact on their lives, transnational identities, and educational experiences.

The reinvention of self (Roces, 2021) is a multi-directional process in that Filipina mothers mobilize the gendered vulnerabilities of the L/CP through their political agency as well. Participating in the global domestic work industry in various nation-states such as Korea, United Arab Emirates, Hong Kong, Japan, Italy, Taiwan, and then ultimately, Canada, Filipina mothers described how they left the lives that they knew in Philippines, including their families and their children, and did whatever it took to give their families and children the best that they could because they did not have opportunities to do so in the Philippines. Rooted within Spanish colonization, beginning from the 16th century and ending in the 19th century, "the most fundamental aspect of Philippine history is the history of the struggles of its people for freedom and a better life" (Constantino & Constantino, 1975, p. 81). These social factors have influenced the migration trajectories of Filipina mothers and their families as most, if not all mothers in the study, expressed that they had left the Philippines for economic reasons. Moreover, this book addresses the "social, economic,...cultural..." (Manalansan, 2006, p. 243) political agency of Filipina mothers as they navigate their migration trajectories and mobilize their gendered vulnerabilities.

Theoretical frameworks

I draw on a range of theoretical frameworks throughout the book which inform my understanding of the impact of the transnational phenomenon of family separation and reunification through Canada's L/CP: (i) Identity and Belonging; (ii) Relational Intersectionality; (iii) Settler Colonialism and Decolonization; and (iv) Transnational Feminism which I elaborate on in subsequent chapters. Here I gesture in shorthand form the significance of each of these frameworks which ground my analytic perspective throughout the book:

i ***Identity and belonging***

Hall (1996) proposed that "identity" is a subjectification process, which entails engaging in political practices of discourse and exclusion that shape identification. Identities are viewed as a construction that is always "'in process'...and lodged in contingency. Once secured, it does not obliterate difference" (pp. 2–3). The process of identification requires the making of symbolic boundaries, requiring "what is left outside, it's constitutive outside, to consolidate the process" (p. 3). This understanding of identity is connected to agency, which is "an ongoing and situated negotiation of self-naming and being named by others that relies on visible and non-visible markers of difference and is implicated in power relations" (Coloma, 2008, p. 20).

These definitions of identity and agency apply to an understanding of how Filipina/o/x youth negotiate their identities in relation to how others define them within the context of Toronto urban schools.

The 'reinvention of self' (Roces, 2021) is situated within the context of political agency, where 'identities' are relationally-constituted within a socio-political context (Hall, 1996), such as Canada's L/CP and the global domestic work industry more broadly. These understandings of identity and agency signify how the "Filipino" identity shifts and changes and is contingent upon global migration trajectories, colonial histories, geographical location, relationships with loved ones, community and friends, and social location as a socio-historically marginalized community. Agency plays an important role as Filipina/o/x youth negotiate these social barriers within these contingencies and as they navigate their belonging in Toronto urban schools. "Belonging" as a concept is understood as both "personal, intimate, [including] feelings of being 'at home' in a place (place-belongingness) and...a discursive resource that constructs, claims, justifies, or resists forms of socio-spatial inclusion/exclusion (politics of belonging)" (Antonsich, 2010, p. 644). Furthermore, Yuval-Davis (2006) argued that "belonging is about emotional attachment, about feeling 'at home'....[whereas] the politics of belonging comprises specific political projects aimed at constructing belonging in particular ways to particular collectivities that are, at the same time, themselves being constructed by these projects in very particular ways. (p. 197)

ii ***Relational intersectionality***

Relational intersectionality goes beyond analyses of intersecting social constructs such as race, class, and gender, to examine resistance, empowerment, and political agency, which are constituted upon oppression and marginalization (Collins, 2019; Coloma, 2008). The chapter analyses how both Filipina mothers and their children navigate the traumas and gendered vulnerabilities of global migration and the role school-community partnerships play.

iii ***Settler colonialism and decolonization***

Settler colonialism and the role that school-community partnerships play in decolonization are explicated in this chapter. In settler colonialism, the role of racialized newcomer as "settlers" and the meaning(s) of decolonization have been contested (Dhamoon, 2015; Garba & Sorentino, 2020; Lawrence & Dua, 2005; Sharma & Wright, 2008; Tuck & Yang, 2012). Therefore, as newcomers migrating to a settler nation-states such as Canada, Filipina/o/x youth and their mothers are implicated in the debates of settler colonialism. Moreover, Indigenous voices may play a significant role in immigration policy (Bauder, 2020; Bauder & Breen, 2022). While this book addresses colonial mentality (David, 2010; 2011; Nadal, 2011) as a form of decolonization, it also examines the role of school-community partnerships in mobilizing the traumas of global migration within a settler-colonial nation-state such as

Canada, educating on solidarity and critical social justice among marginalized communities.

iv ***Transnational feminism***

Lastly, this book utilizes transnational feminism, a theory that focuses on advocacy and activism beyond borders and builds upon solidarities among marginalized communities within a global context (Mohanty, 2003; Nagar & Swarr, 2010). This theoretical framework addresses how school-community partnerships can be used as a tool to engage in advocacy for marginalized students in school and in the community, thereby impacting educational policy and practice.

Mobilizing the traumas of family separation and reunification and gendered vulnerabilities through political agency

Given the economic need for migration, what consequence(s) then would this have on the transnational family dynamic? This book navigates the complexities of family separation and reunification, highlighting the spaces of empowerment (Collins, 2019) among Filipina mothers and their children. On the one hand, it identifies the ways in which Filipina mothers and their children experience the gendered vulnerabilities and traumas of migration, respectively, while on the other, it speaks to the "resistance and agency" (Rother, 2017, p. 957) among these reunified transnational families. The documented educational experiences of many Filipina/o/x youth have been troubling, where high drop-out rates and poor educational outcomes are rampant among those who have experienced family separation and reunification through the L/CP (Caro, 2008; Farrales & Pratt, 2012; Kelly, 2014; Kelly et al., 2014; Pratt, 2010; 2012). Nevertheless, school-community partnerships have been catalysts in educating Filipina/o/x youth about engaging in acts of solidarity and activism, particularly with Indigenous Peoples in Canada and in challenging anti-Black racism in daily social relations.

Moreover, Filipina/o/x youth have deepened their understandings of how their mothers' love runs transnational deep as she does what it takes to support her family as an in/visible[3], marginal subject working mainly global cities[4]. Upon family reunification, Filipina mothers continue to work multiple jobs for their families, while being misunderstood by the educational system and their own children (Kelly, 2014; Pratt, 2010; 2012; Ticar, 2017).

Notwithstanding these gendered vulnerabilities and traumas of family separation and reunification, this book highlights their *political agency,* which is defined as, "an ongoing and situated negotiation of self-naming and being named by others that relies on visible and non-visible markers of difference and is implicated in power relations" (Coloma, 2008, p. 20). It amplifies the voices and advocacy needs of Filipina mothers, their children, and their communities, illuminating how they mobilize the gendered vulnerabilities and traumas of migration through the spaces of *resistance* and *empowerment* (Collins, 2019). Acts of resistance and empowerment among marginalized communities challenge colonial theories, research, and methodology that focus on *damaged-centred research* (Tuck, 2009) and instead, they centre the ways in which power relations are located *within* these communities, not outside (Tuck, 2009; 2010). Political agency occurs in *relationally constituted* ways where experiences of the exploitation, abuse, gendered vulnerabilities, and traumas through the L/CP are analysed through a relational and intersectional approach. While some of the Filipina/o/x youth and their mothers did not necessarily engage in direct "political" conversations, they overtly highlighted how family separation and reunification has impacted their transnational families and lives. With Filipina/o/x youth, school-partnerships have facilitated "a variety of political discourses through which critical understandings are developed" (Hörschelmann & El Refaie, 2014, p. 450), engaging the students in critical social justice.

Centring embodied knowledge[5] in critical social justice research

School-community partnerships have played a critical role in illuminating the *embodied knowledge* of transnational Filipina/o/x youth, particularly when it comes to deep understanding (s) of critical social justice. Critical social justice may be defined as an ongoing commitment towards eradicating injustice based on unequal social and power relations through critical reflection and action (Bondy et al., 2022; Freire, 1970; Sensoy & DiAngelo, 2017). As school-community partnerships engage in critical social justice and the embodied knowledge of Filipina/o/x youth, they also work with the youth in facilitating their political agency. Within the context of transformative and critical social justice, agency may be described as the "commitment to an understanding of the dynamic and dialectical nature of the interaction between individual and social context, and the active role of the individual in the process of identity construction" (Le Roux & Francis, 2011, p. 301). Moreover, the role of school-community partnerships in this particular context has been to engage with Filipina/o/x youth in social justice education around im/migration rights, specifically around the L/CP, a policy and program that has impacted their education experiences and lives.

The role of school-community partnerships in this case, then reflects the need to illuminate the *self-determination*[6] of Filipina/o/x youth and they come to deeper understandings about social injustices that impact their transnational families; their experiences of migration and the 'traumas' of family separation and reunification; and their mothers' gendered vulnerabilities. Diaz-Strong et al. (2014) argue that self-determination is the "right of people to shape their own political and personal pathways" (p. 226). Moreover, *collectivization* is the process whereby "individuals become stronger, … [address potential harm], and develop vocabularies and strategies for personal and political transformation through collectivization" (Diaz-Strong et al., 2014). Critical social justice must be collectively built-in communities where everyone is constantly reminded that power relations and oppressive factors are not static and are ever-changing (Diaz-Strong et al., 2014). The making of critical social justice based on youth resistance "*with* and *by* youth, generates new methodologies, new ethics, and new theory" (Guishard & Tuck, 2014, p. 192). This understanding of youth resistance, in collaboration with school-community partnerships, challenges "colonial [theories] of change that locates power outside of communities" (Guishard & Tuck, 2014, p. 190). Thus, school-community partnerships may play a significant role in decolonization as they work with the youth, and by extension, their mothers, in facilitating their political agency and transmuting the notions, stereotypes, and internalizations of powerlessness, which are the remnants of systemic oppression, colonization, and global migration through Canada's L/CP.

The impact of colonization on global migration

The current global migration processes have had deep roots within the legacy of colonialism in the Philippines. From 1521 to 1898, the Philippines was one of Spain's colonies. In 1898, a war between the United States and Spain over Cuba occurred and Filipina/o/xs believed that the United States was an ally in their revolution against Spain (McElhinny et al., 2012). However,

> Spain, rather than surrendering to [Filipina/o/x] revolutionaries, ceded the Philippines to the United States for twenty million dollars. The United States retained formal sovereignty until the end of Second World War. U.S colonization led to…labour migration…The spectre of U.S. imperialism in the Philippines continues to haunt Filipina/o/[x] lives….in the diaspora's relationship to the Philippines itself" (McElhinny et al., 2012, p. 13).

Besides becoming independent from American colonialization in 1946 and from Spain in 1898, the Philippines had also become independent from Japan in 1943 (Bankoff & Weekley, 2002). Subsequently, "a poverty-breeding society was nurtured…and…the government was burdened with a type of foreign aid which insured that the debtor would be in constant debt to the creditor" (Constantino & Constantino, 1975, p. 394). Global financial institutions, such as the World Bank and the International Monetary Fund (IMF), are seen as "global disciplining regime[s]" (Sassen, 2016, p. 209), implementing Structural Adjustment Programs and lending money to countries in the Global South (Sassen, 2016), such as the Philippines. However, these countries had remained in debt, "even before the economic crisis of the mid-1990s, the debt of poor countries in the South had grown from US $67 billion in 1980 to US $1.4 trillion in 1992" (Sassen, 2016, p. 208). While some global migrations are marked by extreme violence, the flows of migration have also been influenced by international development policies from the last 30 years as "the natural resources of much of Africa and good parts of Latin America and Asia count more than the people on those lands count as consumers and as workers" (Sassen, 2016, p. 207).

During the early 1970s, the government in the Philippines joined the global market through labour export to reduce under/unemployment and alleviate foreign debt through migrants' remittances (Tyner, 1999, p. 679). President Marcos created the Philippine Labour Export Policy through the Ministry of Labour as means to address poverty and lack of employment, which produced the outflow of migrant workers (Migrante, Ottawa). In 2018, the Philippines owed foreign debt in the amount of $76.4 billion USD; as such, the remittances received from labour exploitation has assisted in maintaining the Philippine economy (Migrante Ottawa, 2022). Filipina mothers who had migrated as Live-in/Caregivers have been part of the overseas migrant workers who remit 1.5 billion Canadian dollars annually to the Philippines, assisting the government in foreign debt repayment and to economically support their families (Friesen, 2011; Kessler & Rother, 2016; Pratt, 2012; Sassen, 2004). Economic migrants often hold stereotypical gendered roles such as males working in "masculine" positions in the Middle East, whereas women from the Philippines worked as domestic workers" (Tyner, 1999). However, feminized labour within a transnational context has "simultaneously challenged and reproduced gender discourses and roles" (Liebers & Kunz, 2018, p. 121). Furthermore, as mothers leave their home through global migration to financially support her family in the domestic care work sector, fathers often take on the household tasks and childcare roles (Lam & Yeoh, 2018). In the next section, I provide a brief overview of the L/CP and its trajectory because it is crucial to understand the local and global factors influencing the feminization of labour and its impact on transnational families.

According to Migrante Ottawa (2022), the Philippines is considered a "rich country" with having large mineral deposits and production of geothermal power. However, almost 65% of the total population were living on 125 pesos per day in 2015, and in 2016, 70% identified that they lived in poverty (Migrante Ottawa, 2022). The National Capital Region (NCR) stipulated that the minimum legal wage in 2018 was 1,196 pesos, though these laws are not enforced, and about 40% of the population have precarious jobs (Migrante Ottawa, 2022).

The trajectory of Live-in/Caregiver Program

In 1973, Temporary Foreign Workers Program (TFWP) was created by the Federal Government of Canada so that employers could hire temporary contract workers from outside the country Canadian workers cannot fulfil these positions; once these contracts have ended, these workers must leave Canada (Canadian Union of Public Employees, 2013; Migrante Ottawa, 2022). Under the TFWP, the live-in/caregiver program, *Foreign Domestic Movement* (FDM), began in 1981, and in 1992, the program was renamed as the *Live-in/Caregiver Program* (the former L/CP) (Migrante Ottawa, 2022). Prior to WWII, mostly European women arrived as permanent residents to fulfil roles as caregivers, while after WWII, the Federal Government of Canada started labour contract programs through two bilateral agreements with Caribbean countries: the West Domestic Scheme in 1955 and the Caribbean Domestic Scheme in 1957, with mainly women ages 18–35 coming from Jamaica and Barbados who could achieve permanent residency after 1 year of temporary work (Migrante Ottawa, 2022).

Between 1992 and 2014, the former L/CP required that caregivers complete 3900 hours within a 24-month period while living in their employers' home, in order to obtain permanent residency for themselves and the family members they would sponsor to come to Canada (Government of Canada, 2020). This period of employment entailed family separation, which ranged from 2 years to typically 6–8 years on average (Kelly et al., 2014; Pratt, 2012), though some youths have experienced a period of separation from 12–13 years (Ticar, 2017). As of 2011, 90% of the L/CP participants had migrated from the Philippines (Friesen, 2011). On November 30, 2014, the L/CP concluded as two new pathways emerged for permanent residency: *Caring for Children Class* and *Caring for People with High Medical Needs Class* on June 18, 2019, where each program had a cap of 2,750 annual applications (Migrante Ottawa, 2022). In these particular caregiver process, the live-in requirement was waived, though participants were required to complete their hours within 48 months, as well as fulfil language, educational, and employment requirements (Government of Canada, 2014). In 2016, there was a total of 112,105 Filipinas who participated in the L/CP (Khanam et al., 2022). On June 18, 2019, two programs were created on June 18, 2019 with permanent residency in mind, where caregivers had the opportunity to bring their family members through open work or study permits: *The Home Child Care Provider Pilot and Home Support Worker Pilot,* with a 1 year instead of 2 year work requirement (Government of Canada, 2023; Migrante Ottawa, 2022). Thus, the study of Filipina/o/x labour migration through the L/CP is indeed significant for understanding the mobilization of gendered vulnerabilities and the traumas of family separation and reunification.

Filipina mothers and political agency

Highlighting the gendered vulnerabilities of global migration through the L/CP honours the experiences of Filipina mothers as it illuminates how they have *mobilized* these experiences through their own voices and acts of advocacy through community organizing (de Leon, 2014; Francisco-Menchavez, 2018; Migrante Ontario, 2022; Tungohan, 2012). Prior to the *Migrant Workers and Overseas Filipinos Act* in 1995, the Philippine Government provided very little protection for migrant workers, such as the case of Flor Contemplacion, a domestic worker in Singapore who was accused of murdering the 4-year-old child she was taking care of and was subsequently executed (Migrante Ottawa, 2022). Due to transnational community organizing, prayer vigils, and petitions, the Philippine Government was summoned to fully protect migrant workers as well as provide resources and services and the *Migrant Workers and Overseas Filipinos Act* emerged, though the Philippine Government has not implemented many of the stipulations of this Act. Despite the vulnerabilities among Filipina caregivers to exploitation and abuse within the L/CP:

> Their activism highlights how political activity is not restricted to citizens… instead Filipina live-in caregivers show that 'personhood' – i.e., the fact that they

are human – matters…Their activism expanded notions of the political; not only did they interact with the state to press for reform or for abolition, they also participated in informal politics through the creation of safe spaces for live-in caregivers (Tungohan, 2012, p. 176). On a transnational level, Filipina caregivers have been engaging in activism to address labour concerns. For example, political activism manifests itself among Filipina caregivers in Singapore through "micro and fragmented ways, given the politically restricted environment" (Amrith, 2018, p. 79). In Barcelona, the labour rights of Filipina caregivers have been upheld through grassroots "efforts, in partnerships with municipal agencies, lawyers and unions" (Amrith, 2018, p. 80). Political agency among Filipina caregivers: Is not merely located in binary opposition to power structures and resistance…these women hold their own feminist notions of what constitutes the progressive, and it is shaped through their experiences of transnational displacement as migrant women in the domestic sector and the kinds of relationships they cultivate. Norms are both transgressed and upheld, thus revealing a more ambivalent picture of agency (Amrith, 2018, p. 80). Thus, I extend this argument to the ways in which Filipina mothers mobilize their experiences of gendered vulnerabilities and its impact on Filipina/o/x's youths' political agency, in relation to how school-community partnerships engage in critical social justice.

The study and research questions

The research on which this book is based sought to provide the perspectives and standpoints of both Filipina mothers and their children with their potential to inform education policy and practice with regards to supporting im/migrant children, specifically Filipina/o/x youth in schools. Indeed, my focus was specifically on the role of school-community partnerships seeking to address following research questions:

1 How do Filipina/o/x youth make sense of their racial identity and belonging in Toronto urban schools?
2 How do Filipina/o/x youth make sense of being "Filipino," and to what extent do social constructs such as gender, race, class, sexuality, spirituality, and religion influence their self-understandings as newcomers?
3 How have the specific global migratory circumstances of family separation and reunification impacted Filipina/o/x youth and their experiences of schooling?
4 How have the experiences of family separation and reunification impacted the identities of Filipina/o/x youth?
5 How do Filipina/o/x youth and their mothers engage in forms political agency within spaces of oppression and marginalization?

These key questions are the tools in which to not only discover the impact of family separation and reunification, i.e., trauma experienced among transnational Filipina/o/x families, but to unpack the role of school-community partnerships in educating and implementing equitable policies and practices. Advocacy, then, becomes the collaborative work of school-community partnerships, Filipina/o/x youth, mothers, and those who provide service(s) with and for these specific communities. Migrant scholars who study family separation and reunification among diverse transnational families argue that the process of family separation and reunification is traumatic (Castañeda & Buck, 2011; Mazzucato & Schans, 2011; Pratt, 2012; Zentgraf & Chinchilla, 2012) as "migrants are not only affected by political and social realities, but also by psychological ones" (Castañeda & Buck, 2011, p. 89). Having social services available to assist transnational families in a culturally-specific manner, such as the services available for the Filipina/o/x community, helps to address the effects of family separation and reunification through the L/CP. Having these organizations address the specific needs of Filipina/o/x youth facilitates the process of utilizing their agency to make sense of their transnational identities in urban schools. Moreover, it is important to acknowledge that individuals experience family separation and reunification through the L/CP differently, "viewing migration as trauma does not mean that all migrants face paralysing emotional pain. Like all traumas, an individual's response is highly dependent on character, maturity, life experience, past responses to traumas and the quality of parenting received" (Castañeda & Buck, 2011, p. 89). School-community partnerships play an important role in informing social services, educational systems, and policy makers to understand how family separation and reunification through the L/CP impacts Filipina/o/x youth.

Moreover, this book draws from my postdoctoral research, which is an extension of this particular my doctoral study (Ticar, 2017), which took place from May 2021 to May 2022. Participants included 1 reunified Filipina mother and 2 children (20 and 22 years old), in which the mother and daughter participated in my doctoral research. Additionally, there was 1 focus group with 2 Filipina/o/x social service providers and 1 individual interview with a Filipina/o/x social service provider who provided their perspectives on anti-racist and anti-oppressive practice (Ocampo & Pino, 2014). My postdoctoral research focused on Filipina mothers and their children, looking deeper into the family system's as well as Filipina/o/x social services providers' perspectives on how to improve social service provision, which has significance for social service provision. The following are the following research questions:

Interview questions for social service providers

1 What is your understanding of anti-racism and/or anti-oppressive practice?
2 What are your equity, diversity, and inclusion policies and how do you implement these?
3 In your services and/or interventions, (without breaking confidentiality) what are the main issues that you see among Filipina/o/x families who have been reunified through Canada's Live- in/Caregiver Program (L/CP)?

4 What are the strengths that the Filipina/o/x families who have experienced reunification through L/CP possess?
5 How does the Filipina/o/x community understand their experiences of family separation and reunification? How do they transform these experiences as a form of empowerment (general experiences, no need to break client/recipient confidentiality)?
6 What types of interventions and/or services do you employ when working with Filipina/o/x families who have experienced family separation and reunification through the L/CP?

Interview questions for Filipina/o/x families

Session 1: Separation period

1 For the youth: what was your experience like when you were separated from your mother/parent?
2 For the former caregiver parent: what was your experience like when you were separated from your children and family?
3 For other family member(s): what was your experience like when you were separated from the former caregiver?
4 For the youth: How was it like to hear the experiences of the former caregiver and other family member(s)?
5 For the former caregiver and family member(s): How was it like to hear the experiences of the youth?

Session 2: During reunification

1 What are some of the memories that you have of family reunification?
2 What were some of the experiences you faced during family reunification? If there were any concerns, how did you overcome them?
3 What were your experiences like when you accessed social services? What did you appreciate, what would you like to see more of (improvement?)
4 How did you learn and grow together as a family who recently reunified?
5 What did you learn about yourselves as individuals? As a family?

Session 3: After reunification

6 What are your hopes and dreams for the future as a family and as individuals?
7 What are your recommendations for the services that you received?
8 Upon reflection, what has helped you adjust to your new family dynamics?
9 How do you continue to build your relationship as a family?
10 How do you continue to learn more about your individual and collective identities as a reunified Filipina/o/x family (in relation to other community members who have had similar experiences?)

Overview of the book

The rest of the chapters in this book excavate deeper into the topics discussed above, particularly with regards to how Filipina/o/x youth and their mothers engage in political agency and mobilize trauma and gendered vulnerabilities in collaboration with school-community partnerships. Chapter 2 examines how my own positionality as author is key to facilitating the political agency of Filipina mothers and their children while introducing the methodology and methods that were used as tools of mobilization. Chapter 3 showcases how Filipina mothers mobilize the gendered vulnerabilities of Filipinas have been transnational migration, specifically that of Canada's Live-in/Caregiver Program (L/CP). It addresses the gendered vulnerabilities of transnational migration through three levels: micro, mezzo, and macro levels. It presents Filipina mothers' experiences of emotional and physical labour from the triangulated perspectives of Filipina/o/x youth and their mothers, as well as community leaders serving Filipina/o/x communities. It outlines how Filipina mothers' gendered vulnerabilities are analysed through relational intersectional framework(s) whereby social categories such as race, class, and gender create hierarchical boundaries in society (Anthias, 2011; Collins, 2019), which prevents the economic mobilization among racialized communities in urban neighbourhoods (Anyon, 2013). Moreover, this chapter illuminates the role of school-community partnerships in addressing social inequities, particularly the socio-economic status of Filipina/o/x youth, their mothers and family members, and their communities.

Chapter 4 provides insight into Filipina/o/x youths' experiences of trauma due to family separation and reunification as a result of Canada's Live-in/Caregiver Program (L/CP) and how they mobilize these traumas through an understanding of their mothers' gendered vulnerabilities (Jaggar, 2009). Chapter 5 explores the ways in which Filipina/o/x youth both individually and collectively make meaning of their intersectional identities and transnational belonging within the context of the their mothers' gendered vulnerabilities (González, 2003; Jones, 2011; Mohanty, 2003). The purpose of this chapter is to examine how the youth engage in their political agency in relation to their experiences of the traumas of family separation and reunification through global migration, specifically the L/CP and the situated and historical impact of colonialism. Moreover, it analyses how school-community partnerships exemplify transnational feminist praxis (Nagar & Swarr, 2010) and decolonization processes (González, 2003; Jones, 2011; Mohanty, 2003). Finally, it examines the ways in which power relations play a part in the construction of intersectional identities (Coloma, 2008) and analyses the legacy of colonialism.

Chapter 6 looks at the continuum of gendered vulnerabilities and the feminization of domestic work on a global level (Jaggar, 2009), from addressing Filipina/o/x youths' settlement needs to building solidarities through allyship when it comes to addressing abuses of the nation-state such as Canada

(Tungohan, 2012). Moreover, this chapter situates these gendered vulnerabilities and feminization of domestic work with the particular context of settler colonialism in Canada and the role of racialized communities in dismantling the continual colonization of Indigenous peoples in Canada (Mahtani & Roberts, 2012). I continue with this conversation of how to dismantle the impact of colonization on Indigenous peoples in Canada by positing that school-community partnerships play a significant role in educational policies and practices that go beyond the classroom and into society. Furthermore, it outlines how transnational feminist praxis within schools, communities, and social services can be used as an advocacy tool to facilitate Filipina/o/x youths' political agency and sense of identity and belonging in urban schools. It highlights the racialized and gendered subjectivities of Filipina/o/x youth and their mothers, and the intersection with their sexual, faith/spiritual, and classed identities. Critical frameworks such as relational intersectionality, settler colonialism and decolonization, and transnational feminism impact advocacy interventions such as public, social, educational, and im/migration programs and policies, so that vulnerable communities can reclaim spaces of marginality (Nagar & Swarr, 2010). Furthermore, school-community partnerships hold a significant role in facilitating decolonization processes that engage Filipina/o/x youths' reflective, emotional, and gendered selves (Mohanty, 2003). As the youth engage in political agency, critical framework(s) such as relational intersectionality, settler colonialism and decolonization, and transnational feminism are utilized to elicit deeper understandings of how school-community partnerships work through decolonization processes and utilize the space to advocate for, and with, Filipina/o/x youth, their mothers, and their communities.

Finally, Chapter 7 posits that systemic racism and oppression as well as the legacy of colonialism have impacted the migratory experiences of transnational racialized women who have left their children behind for economic migration. These children, such as the Filipina/o/x youth in the study, have experienced traumas, specifically due to systemic racism and their mothers' global migration experiences in domestic work (Pratt, 2012). These were expressed through feelings of depression and loneliness due to the im/migration policies of the L/CP. Thus, their experiences of trauma and expressed emotions have advocacy implications in that their micro realities are connected to the macro political factors of global migration (Zembylas, 2012). Moreover, this study points to other potential roles that school-community partnerships could play in educational policy, such as financially supporting families with low income (Anyon, 2013). Therefore, school-community partnerships, and the social relations therein, are the advocacy sites upon which Filipina/o/x youth negotiate political agency and systemic racism, having an impact on the broader Canadian community and im/migration policies. Furthermore, recommendations for im/migration and educational policies are identified in this chapter.

Notes

1 Now currently called "Home Child Care Provider Pilot and Home Support Worker Pilot programs" as of June 18, 2019 (Immigration, Refugees, and Citizenship Canada, 2023).
2 I have opted for the use of 'Filipina/o/x' rather than solely using 'Filipinx' (Nadal, 2019), in which the latter is a contested term (Cabigao, 2021), to provide space for the youth to identify themselves. 'Filipina' mainly refers to 'female', 'Filipino mostly means 'male', and 'Filipinx' is a term that refers to all genders.
3 The hypervisibility of the Filipina/o/x community is highlighted in stereotypes, but they remain invisible in other social aspects, such as when achievements are ignored (McElhinny et al., 2012).
4 In global cities, there are two main labour demands: high-waged transnational professionals and low-waged domestic workers, mainly women im/migrants (Sassen, 2008).
5 Embodied knowledge refers to the "imprint of students' emotions, experiences, and histories in their bodies" (Bondy et al., 2022).
6 See Diaz-Strong et al. (2014) in the reference list.

References

Amrith, M. (2018). Dignity of labour: Activism among Filipina domestic workers in Singapore and Barcelona. In R. Nagar, & A. L. Swarr (Eds.), *Critical transnational feminist praxis* (pp. 166–191). State University of New York Press.

Anthias, F. (2011). Intersections and translocations: New paradigms for thinking about cultural diversity and social identities. *European Educational Research Journal, 10*(2), 204–217.

Anthias, F. (2012). Intersectional what? Social divisions, intersectionality and levels of analysis. *Ethnicities, 13*(1), 3–19.

Antonsich, M. (2010). Searching for belonging: An analytical framework. *Geography Compass, 4*(6), 644–659.

Anyon, J. A. (2013). Political economy of race, urban education, and educational policy. In C. McCarthy, W. Crichlow, G. Dimitriadis, & N. Dolby (Eds.), *Race, identity, and representation in education,* (2nd ed.) (pp. 369–378).

Anzaldúa, G. (1999). *Borderlands/La frontera* (2nd ed.). Aunt Lute Books.

Bakker, C., Elings-Pels, M., & Reis, M. (2009). *The impact of migration on children in the Caribbean.* UNICEF.

Bankoff, G., & Weekley, K. (2002). *Post-colonial national identity in the Philippines: Celebrating the centennial of independence.* Ashgate.

Barndt, D. (2010). Remapping the Americas: A transnational engagement with creative tensions of community arts. In R. Nagar, & A. L. Swarr (Eds.), *Critical transnational feminist praxis* (pp. 166–191). State University of New York Press.

Bauder, H. (2020). Migrant solidarities and the politics of place. *Progress in Human Geography, 44*(6), 1066–1080. https://doi.org/10.1177/0309132519876324

Behar, R. (1996). *The vulnerable observer: Anthropology that breaks your heart.* Beacon.

Bernal, D. D. (1998). Using a chicana feminist epistemology in educational research. *Harvard Educational Review, 68*(4), 555–582.

Brah, A. (2003). Diaspora, border and transnational identities. In R. Lewis, & S. Mills (Eds.), *Feminist postcolonial theory: A reader* (pp. 613–634). Edinburgh University Press.

Bauder, & Breen (2022), H. (2011). Closing the immigration–Aboriginal parallax gap. *Geoforum*, *42*(5), 517–519. https://doi.org/10.1016/j.geoforum.2011.03.007.
Bondy, Burt, E., & Bell, P. V. (2022). Cultivating critical social justice literacy: Surfacing and examining Candidates' embodied knowledge. *The New Educator*, *18*(1-2), 27–41. https://doi.org/10.1080/1547688X.2021.1982096
Castañeda, & Buck (2011). Remittances, transnational parenting, and the children left behind: Economic and psychological implications. *The Latin Americanist*, *55*, 85–110.
Chase, R.M., Medina, M.F. & Mignone, J. (2012). The life story board: A feasibility study of a visual interview tool for school counsellors. Canadian Journal of Counselling and Psychotherapy /Revue canadienne de counseling et de psychothérapie 46(3), 183–200.
Cabigao, K. (2021, January 7). Are you Filipino or Filipinx? *VICE*. https://www.vice.com/en/article/qjpwnm/filipino-vs-filipinx-debate-language-Philippines-culture-identity
Canadian Union of Public Employees. (2013). *Fact sheet: Temporary Foreign Workers Program*. Retrieved from: https://cupe.ca/fact-sheet-temporary-foreign-workers-program
Caro, J. F. (2008). The Educational Experiences of Filipino Youth in Quebec in the Context of Global Migration (Master's thesis). Retrieved from ProQuest Dissertations and Theses database. (Assession Order No. MR66914). https://escholarship.mcgill.ca/concern/theses/pr76f729d
Chung, M. M. L. (2012). *The relationships between racialized immigrants and indigenous peoples in Canada: A literature review*. Ryerson University Toronto.
Collins, P. H. (2019). *Intersectionality as critical social theory*. Duke University Press.
Coloma, R. S. (2008). Border crossing subjectivities and research: Through the prism of feminists of color. *Race, Ethnicity, and Education*, *11*(1), 11–27.
Conquergood, L. D. (2013). In E.P Johnson (Ed.), *Cultural struggles: Performance, ethnography, praxis*. University of Michigan.
Constantino, R., & Constantino, L. R. (1975). *A history of the Philippines: From the Spanish colonization to the second world war*. Monthly Review Press.
Creswell, J. W. (2013). *Qualitative inquiry and research design: Choosing among five approaches*. SAGE.
Curley, G., Lookabaugh, L., Neubert, C., & Smith, S. (2022). Decolonisation is a political project: Overcoming impasses between indigenous sovereignty and abolition. *Antipode*, *54*(4), 1043–1062. https://doi.org/10.1111/anti.12830
David, E. J. R. (2010). Cultural mistrust and mental health help-seeking attitudes among Filipino Americans. *Asian American Journal of Psychology*, *1*(1), 57–66. https://doi.org/10.1037/a0018814
David, E. J. R. (2011). *Filipino-American Postcolonial psychology: Oppression colonial mentality and decolonization*. Authorhouse.
David, E. J. R. (2013). *Brown skin, white minds: Filipino-/American postcolonial psychology* (with commentaries). Information Age Publishing.
de Jesús, M. L. (2005). *Pinay power: Peminist critical theory: Theorizing the Filipina/American experience*. Routledge.
de Leon, C. (2014). Family separation and reunification among former Filipina migrant domestic workers and their adult daughters in two Canadian. In cities in M. Romero, V. Preston, & W. Giles (Eds.), *When care work Goes global: Locating the social relations of domestic work* (pp. 139–158). Ashgate.
Dhamoon, R. K. (2015). A feminist approach to decolonizing anti-racism: Rethinking transnationalism, intersectionality, and settler colonialism. *Feral Feminisms*, *4*, 20–37.https://feralfeminisms.com/wp-content/uploads/2015/12/ff_A-Feminist Approach-to-Decolonizing-Anti-Racism_issue4.pdf
Diaz-Strong, D., Gómez, C., Luna-Duarte, M., & Meiners, E. R. (2014). Out for immigration justice: Thinking through social and political change. In E. Tuck, & K. W. Yang (Eds.), *Youth resistance research and theories of change* (pp. 218–229). Routledge.

Dillard, C. B., & Okapalaoka, C. (2011). The sacred and spiritual nature of endarkened transnational feminist praxis in qualitative research. In N. K. Denzin, & Y. S. Lincoln (Eds.), *SAGE handbook of qualitative research* (pp. 147–162). SAGE.

Ellingson, L. L. (2011). Analysis and representation across the continuum. In N. K. Denzin, & Y. S. Lincoln (Eds.), *SAGE handbook of qualitative research* (pp. 595–610). SAGE.

Erikson, F. (2011). A history of qualitative inquiry in social and educational research. In N.K Denzin & Y.S Lincoln (Eds.), *SAGE Handbook of Qualitative Research* (pp. 43–59). SAGE.

Farrales, M., & Pratt, G. (2012). Stalled development of immigrant Filipino youths: Migration, suspended ambitions and the ESL classroom. *Metropolis British Columbia Centre of Excellence for Research on Immigration and Diversity. Working Paper Series* (Working Papers Series No. 12-10). Metropolis British Columbia.

Finley, S. (2011). Critical arts-based inquiry: The pedagogy and performance of a radicalethical aesthetic. In N. Denzin, & Y. Lincoln (Eds.), *The SAGE handbook of qualitative research* (pp. 435–450). SAGE.

Francisco-Menchavez (2018). *The labor of care: Filipina migrants and transnational families in the digital age*. University of Illinois Press.

Freire, P. (1970). *Pedagogy of the oppressed.* Continuum.

Friesen, J. (2011). *The Philippines now Canada's top source of immigrants*. Globe and mail. Retrieved from: http://www.theglobeandmail.com/news/national/the-philippines-now-canadas-top-source-of-immigrants/article573133/.

Garba, T., & Sorentino, S. (2020). Slavery is a metaphor: A critical commentary on eve tuck and k. Wayne Yang's "Decolonization is not a metaphor. *Antipode*, *52*(3), 764–782. https://doi.org/10.1111/anti.12615

González, M. C. (2000). The four seasons of ethnography: A creation-centred ontology for ethnography. *International Journal of Intercultural Relations*, *24*, 623–650.

González, M. C. (2003). An ethics for postcolonial ethnography. In R. P. Clair (Ed.), *Expressions of ethnography: Novel approaches to qualitative methods* (pp. 77–86). State University of New York.

Government of Canada. (2014). *Improving Canada's Caregiver Program.* Retrieved from: https://www.canada.ca/en/news/archive/2014/10/improving-canada-caregiver-program-898729.html

Government of Canada. (2020). *Live-In Caregiver Program: About the process* Retrieved from: https://www.canada.ca/en/immigration-refugees-citizenship/services/work-canada/hire-permanent-foreign/caregiver-program.html

Government of Canada. (2023). *The Home Child Care Provider Pilot and Home Support Worker Pilot.* Retrieved from: https://www.canada.ca/en/immigration-refugees-citizenship/services/immigrate-canada/caregivers/child-care-home-support-worker.html

Guishard, M., & Tuck, E. (2014). Youth resistance research methods and ethical challenges. In E. Tuck, & K. W. Yang (Eds.), *Youth resistance research and theories of change* (pp. 181–194). Routledge.

Hall, S. (1996). Introduction: Who needs 'identity'? In P. du Gay & H. Hall (Eds.), *Questions of cultural identity*, (pp. 1–17). SAGE. https://doi.org/10.4135/9781446221907

Hörschelmann, K., & El Refaie, E. (2014). Transnational citizenship, dissent and the political geographies of youth. *Transactions of the Institute of British Geographers*, *39*(3), 444–456. 10.1111/tran.12033.

Jaggar, A. M. (2009). Transnational cycles of gendered vulnerability: A prologue to a theory of global gender justice. *Global Gender Justice*, *37*(2), 33–52.

Janesick, V. J. (2010). *Oral History for the qualitative researcher: Choreographing the story*. Guilford Press.

Johnson, E. P. (2013). Introduction: "Opening and interpreting lives. In E. P. Johnson (Ed.), *Cultural struggles: Performance, ethnography, praxis* (pp. 1–14). University of Michigan.

Jones, R. B. (2011). *Postcolonial representations of women*. Springer.

Kelly, P. (2014). *Understanding intergenerational social mobility: Filipino Youth in Canada. IRPP study* 45. Institute for Research on Public Policy.

Kelly, P. F., Austria, J., Chua, J., de Leon, C., Esguerra, E., Felipe, A., & Tupe, E. (2014). *Promoting post-secondary pathways among Filipino youth in Ontario*. York Centre for Asian Research, York University and Community Alliance for Social Justice.

Kessler, C., & Rother, S. (2016). *Democratization through migration?: Political remittances and participation of Philippine return migrants*. Lexington Books.

Khanam, F., Langevin, M., Savage, K., & Uppal, S. (2022, January 25). *Women working in paid care occupations*. Statistics Canada. Retrieved August 23, 2022 from: https://www150.statcan.gc.ca/n1/pub/75-006-x/2022001/article/00001-eng.htm

Lam, T., & Yeoh, B. S. A. (2018). Migrant mothers, left-behind fathers: The negotiation of gender subjectivities in Indonesia and the Philippines. *Gender, Place and Culture: A Journal of Feminist Geography*, *25*(1), 104–117. https://doi.org/10.1080/0966369X.2016.1249349

Lawrence, B., & Dua, E. (2005). Decolonizing anti-racism. *Social Justice*, *32*(4), 120–143.

Le Roux, A., & Francis, D. (2011). Teaching for social justice education: The intersection between identity, critical agency, and social justice education. *South African Journal of Education*, *31*(3), 299–311. https://doi.org/10.15700/saje.v31n3a533

Lee, H. (2016). 'I was forced here': Perceptions of agency in second generation 'return' migration to Tonga. *Journal of Ethnic and Migration Studies*, *42*(15), 2573–2588. doi: 10.1080/1369183X.2016.1176524.

Liebers, M. J. O., & Kunz, S. (2018). Gender roles and relations within Bolivian migrant networks: Ambivalent transgressions, regressions and new autonomies. In M. Amrith, & N. Sahraoui (Eds.), *Gender, work and migration: Agency in gendered labour settings* (pp. 121–139). Routledge.

Madison, D. S. (2005). *Critical ethnography: Method, ethics, and performance*. SAGE.

Madison, D. S. (2012). *Critical ethnography: Method, ethics, and performance* (2nd ed.). SAGE.

Mahtani, M., & Roberts, D. (2012). Contemplating new spaces in Canadian studies. In R. S. Coloma, B. McElhinny, E. Tungohan, J. P. C. Cantugal, & L. M. Davidson (Eds.), *Filipinos in Canada: Disturbing invisibility* (pp. 417–426). University of Toronto.

Manalansan, M. F. (2006). Queer intersections: Sexuality and gender in migration studies. *International Migration Review*, *40*(1), 224–249.

Mazzucato, V., & Schans, D. (2011). Transnational families and the well-being of children: Conceptual and methodological challenges. *Journal of Marriage and Family*, *73*, 704–712.

McElhinny, B., Davidson, L. M., Cantugal, J. P. C., Tungohan, E., & Coloma, R. S. (2012). Spectres of (in)visibility: Filipina/o labour, culture and youth in Canada. In R. S. Coloma, B. McElhinny, E. Tungohan, J. P. C. Cantugal, & L. M. Davidson (Eds.), *Filipinos in Canada: Disturbing invisibility* (pp. 5–45). University of Toronto Press.

Migrante Ottawa. (2022). *Filipino Migrants in Ottawa*. Retrieved August 23, 2022 from http://migranteottawa.org.

Mohanty, C. T. (2003). *Feminism without borders: Decolonizing theory, practicing solidarity*. Duke University Press.

Nadal, K. [@kevinnadal]. (2019, July 3). *#DearFilipinoAmericans*. Twitter. https://twitter.com/kevinnadal/status/1146502369712254976?lang=en

Nadal, K. L. (2011). *Filipino American Psychology: A handbook of theory, research, and clinical practice*. John Wiley & Sons. https://doi.org/10.1002/9781118094747

Nagar, R., & Swarr, A. L. (2010). *Critical transnational feminist praxis*. State University of New York Press.
Ocampo, M., & Pino, F. L. (2014). Developing mental health services: The myth of 'Global' mental health. In R. Moodley, & M. Ocampo (Eds.), *Critical psychiatry and mental health: exploring the work of Suman Fernando in clinical practice* (pp. 145–155). The University of Chicago Press.
Pascale, C. M. (2011). *Cartographies of knowledge: Exploring qualitative epistemologies*. SAGE.
Pierce, L. M. (2005). Not just my closet: Exposing familial, cultural, and imperial skeletons. In M. L. de Jesús (Ed.), *Pinay power: Peminist critical theory: Theorizing the Filipina/American experience* (pp. 31–44). Routledge.
Pratt, G. (2010). Listening for spaces of ordinariness: Filipino-Canadian youths' transnational lives. *Children's Geographies*, *8*(4), 343–352.
Pratt, G. (2012*). Families apart: Migrant mothers and conflicts of labour and love*. University of Minnesota Press.
Regan, P. (2010). *Unsettling the settler within*. UBC Press.
Roces, M. (2021). *The Filipino migration experience global agents of change*. Cornell University Press. https://doi.org/10.1515/9781501760426
Rother, S. (2017). Indonesian Migrant domestic workers in transnational political spaces: Agency, gender roles and social class formation. *Journal of Ethnic and Migration Studies*, *43*(6), 956–973. https://doi.org/10.1080/1369183X.2016.1274567
Sassen, S. (2004). Global cities and survival circuits. In Ehrenreich, B., & Hochschild, A.R (Eds.). *Global Woman: Nannies, Maids, and Sex Workers in the New Economy* (pp. 254–274). Henry Holt and Company.
Sassen, S. (2008). Two stops in today's new global geographies: Shaping novel labour supplies and employment regimes. *American Behavioral Scientist*, *52*(3), 457–496.
Sassen, S. (2016). A massive loss of habitat: New drivers for migration. *Sociology of Development*, *2*(2), 204–233.
Scott, D., & Morrison, M. (2007). *Key ideas in educational research*. Continuum.
Sensoy, O., & DiAngelo, R. (2017). *Is everyone really equal? An introduction to key concepts in social justice education* (2nd ed.). Teachers College Press.
Sharma, N., & Wright, C. (2008). Decolonizing resistance: Challenging colonial states. *Social Justice*, *35*(3), 120–138.
Shopes, L. (2011). Oral History. In N. Denzin, & Y. Lincoln (Eds.), *The SAGE handbook of qualitative research* (pp. 451–466). SAGE.
Taylor, P., & Murphy, C. (2013). *Catch the fire: An art-full guide to unleashing the creative power of youth, adults and communities*. New Society Publishers.
Thomas, J. (1993). *Doing critical ethnography*. SAGE.
Ticar, J. E. (2017). Investigating the transnational identities of Filipina/o/x youth in Toronto urban high schools: A critical ethnographic study of the impact of Canada's live-in/caregiver program [Doctoral dissertation, University of Western Ontario]. Scholarship@Western. https://ir.lib.uwo.ca/etd/4951
Tuck, E. (2009). Suspending damage: A letter to communities. *Harvard Educational Review*, *79*(3), 409–428.
Tuck, E. (2010). Breaking up with Deleuze: Desire and valuing the irreconcilable. *International Journal of Qualitative Studies in Education*, *23*(5), 635–650.
Tuck, E., & Yang, K. W. (2012). Decolonization is not a metaphor. *Decolonization: Indigeneity, Education & Society*, *1*(1), 1–40. https://jps.library.utoronto.ca/index.php/des/article/view/18630/15554
Tungohan, E. (2012). Debunking notions of migrant 'Victimhood': A critical assessment of temporary labour migration programs and Filipina migrant activism in Canada. In

R. S. Coloma, B. McElhinny, E. Tungohan, J. P. C. Cantugal, & L. M. Davidson (Eds.), *Filipinos in Canada: Disturbing invisibility* (pp. 161–80). University of Toronto.

Tyner, J. A. (1999). The global context of gendered labor migration from the Philippines to the United States. *American Behavioural Scientist, 42(*4), 671–689.

Vidaview Information Systems Ltd. (2022). *The Vidaview Life Story Board™: An Innovative and Versatile Therapy, Interview, and Assessment Tool.* https://www.facebook.com/lifestoryboard

Yuval-Davis, N. (2006). Belonging and the politics of belonging. *Patterns of Prejudice, 40*(3), 197–214.

Zembylas, M. (2012). Transnationalism, migration and emotions: Implications for education. *Globalisation, Societies and Education, 10*(2), 163–179.

Zentgraf, K. M., & Chinchilla, N. S. (2012). Transnational family separation: A framework for analysis. *Journal of Ethnic and Migration Studies, 38*(2), 345–366. doi: 10.1080/1369183X.2011.646431.

2 Witnessing political agency as co-performer through the arts

> I know of the Philippines, but it is also so foreign to me. My whole body has been affected by my family's migration to Canada, even though I was born and raised here, but the legacy of my parents' experiences is my story too, and their firsthand experiences of racism haunt me... I am rooted and have been uprooted from my roots...but my strength lies in my heart and mind as I work with tools to transform society. In my heart is my community, my loved ones, and the youth that I have worked with on such an emotionally intimate level. My hands are creative and I constantly create... My feet symbolize migration and my transnational roots and my own process of identity and belonging, which is still in the making
>
> (Fieldnotes, April 16, 2016)

From May 2016 to February 2017, I built some of the most significant and important relations within Filipina/o/x organizations such as the Newcomer Support Centre (NSC)[1] and the Services for a Diverse Community (SDC)[2]. I had also built key mutually trusting relationships with Filipina mothers and their children and Filipina/o/x community leaders during this time. In May 2016, Filipina/o/x leaders welcomed me to NSC and I participated in their school programmes in Toronto, which is a school-community partnership. To gain broader understanding of how Filipina/o/x youth and their mothers utilized their political agency as well as the role of Filipina/o/x community leaders, I began my work with the SDC on September 16, 2016 as they were also engaged with school-community partnerships in Toronto urban schools. Throughout my fieldwork, I engaged with the Filipina/o/x leaders in after-school programmes, which were mostly spoken in Tagalog, and because I understand the language, there were very little barriers to communication. This was a pivotal moment for me in that the youth were provided the environment to speak in the language(s) they most resonated with, where English was not a privileged language in this transnational and sacred[3] space. Filipina/o/x leaders provided opportunities to facilitate space for youth to showcase their political agency, where they had entry points in Toronto urban schools to engage in meaningful negotiations of their transnational identities within Toronto urban schools. The youth indicated

DOI: 10.4324/9781003287469-2

that art, dance, and trips would benefit their overall connection with community and one another. Thus, the use of art was a key factor in my collaboration with Filipina/o/x youth to facilitate their voices as advocacy sites.

Situating myself as 'co-performer'[4] in critical ethnography

Collaborating with the Filipina/o/x community in Toronto, particularly with community leaders, was also a central part in facilitating the political agency of Filipina mothers and their children. Drawing from the *Four Sources of Cultural Intuition*[5] (Bernal, 1998) as 'co-performer', I connected my personal experiences and cultural memories through community knowledge such as kuwentuhans (talk-story) to my own professional experiences as a counsellor in community mental health agencies and to the analytical research process. Critical ethnography provided the space to shed light on the spirit of transformative research, holding this work with sacredness (Dillard & Okapaloka, 2011) with the Filipina/o/x community in Toronto. Dillard and Okapaloka (2011) understood that "*spirituality* is to have a consciousness of the realm of spirit in one's work and to recognize that consciousness as a transformative force in research and teaching" (emphasis in the original) (p. 155). The *sacred* refers to "*the way the work is honoured and embraced as it [is] carried out*...work that is worthy of being held with *reverence* as it is done" (emphasis in original) (Dillard & Okapaloka, 2011, pp. 148–149). I also held in reverence my role as a *vulnerable observer* (Behar, 1996) whose vulnerability was at the centre of my relations with the Filipina/o/x community as opposed to detached. Ultimately, this produced moments of encountering the knowledge(s) and lived experiences that "[broke my] heart" (Behar, 1996, p. 161), which then mobilized these processes within our "relations of solidarity" (Erikson, 2011, p. 51) within this critical ethnography.

Like traditional ethnography, critical ethnography entails doing fieldwork at [a] particular site[s] in order to gather data on the cultural behaviours, meanings, and rich insights of the participants of the study (Scott & Morrison, 2007). Traditional ethnography tends to speak for and/or about the participants while critical ethnography *centres* the voices of the participants for the purpose of engaging in acts of solidary for social action and change (Thomas, 1993). In critical ethnography, its advocacy role provides a connective link between the data gathered from the local to the global, evaluating the disruption of seemingly neutral knowledge(s). Additionally, critical ethnography sheds light on existing power relations where researchers utilize their privilege to dismantle the oppressive social structures impacting marginalized communities (Madison, 2012). Critical ethnographic investigations go beyond fact verification and synthesize the "memory, yearnings, polemics, and hope that are unveiled and inseparable from shared and inherited expressions of communal strivings, social history, and political possibility" (Madison, 2012, p. 29). Thus, this book highlights how these cultural knowledge(s) have been co-produced with Filipina mothers, their children, and Filipina/o/x community leaders, including myself as an author and co-performer.

Vulnerability in the field

As a vulnerable observer (Behar, 1996), emotions, the spiritual, the scared, the circular rather than the linear (González, 2000), were at the forefront when engaging with the Filipina/o/x community and Filipina mothers and their children. Moreover, I embraced (2012) "the emotions and sensuality of *what* is being described through highlighting, sometimes redescribing, the remembered textures, smells, sounds, tastes, and sights rendered through story and performance" (emphasis in original) (p. 36). During fieldwork, I was completely immersed in my senses I smelled and tasted food; I heard music and conversations in Tagalog, other Filipino languages and English; I saw laughter, shyness, openness, dancing, and tears; and I touched pen, paper, and markers to mark my insider/outsider status through artwork. As an insider, I felt a sense of belonging as a member of the Filipina/o/x community in Toronto. However, as an outsider, I was a witness to the youths' experiences of family separation and reunification through the L/CP. As I was born in Canada and have not experienced family separation and reunification through the L/CP, I was an outsider whose privilege lies in the fact that I was an academic in these particular transnational spaces. On October 11, 2016, I noted key points, some of which are as follows:

> I found NSC and great school settlement workers who have office space at the school and who run their programs within the school setting. I was introduced to students at lunch at the cafeteria and tomorrow I will be participating in their after-school program led by the NSC facilitators. It's great that the students can just walk into the office and feel safe in doing so. One Filipino student just opened up to the settlement workers and said that he thinks that he is bisexual. I also like how there are programs for all newcomer students, but also how there are culturally-specific ones too. The settlement workers are attentive to the needs of the students, providing them with snacks, juice, and a listening ear. When it came to the interviews, I was surprised about how open the students were talking about their lives and their emotions. I feel like they were waiting for someone to just ask them about how it was like to be separated from their mothers for so long.
>
> (October 11, 2016)

It is important to note that there were a variety of referral, information, health, and social supports for the Filipina/o/x community, particularly for the youth, as they navigate their lives in educational and social spaces. Both NSC and SDC as community organizations that have school-community partnerships seemed to facilitate the space for Filipina/o/x youth to make sense of their transnational identities in terms of gender, race, ethnicity, class, sexuality, spirituality, and religion, providing opportunities to address global migration processes (Mohanty, 2003) through the L/CP.

Anzaldúa (1999) posited that Mexico, her homeland, is part of "the Third World that grates against the first and bleeds…[and] the lifeblood of two worlds merge to form a third country – a border culture" (p. 25). This 'border culture' also represents possibilities for transformation, particularly in the ways in which school-community partnerships facilitated the political agency of Filipina mothers and their children. Moreover, this study highlighted "strategies for change" (Pierce, 2005, p. 37) through creative arts methods, shedding light on how the "the concept of diaspora should be understood in terms of historically contingent 'genealogies' in the Foucauldian sense, that is, as an ensemble of investigative technologies that historicise trajectories of different diasporas, and analyse their relationality across fields of social relations, subjectivity, and identity" (Brah, 2003, pp. 614–615).

Notes from the field

Like the NSC, the SDC works with diverse newcomer communities through culturally specific programming. Unlike the NSC, SDC's the school settlement workers are located within Toronto urban schools, thus making it more accessible for students to come to the office during lunch and after school. If the students were having a difficult time in the classroom, teachers often sent them to the SDC office for further support. Guidance counsellors also worked closely with the school settlement workers, particularly when encountering concerns with newcomer students. The SDC works with a variety of age groups, including the early years (below 5 years old) and offers English language learning at their sites. Settlement workers are also situated in local libraries as their form of outreach to newcomers. The SDC engages in technology through Digital Storytelling to reach out to families, youth, and others in the community. The purpose of Digital Storytelling is for newcomers of all ages to share their migration stories or any story they would like to share with the community. In schools, teachers have also been adopting this method as a way to relate to their students. In terms of community policies, the SDC engages with partner organizations to gather people to talk about things that matter and as a way to be active and engaged in politics and in society.

As a participant-observer and co-performer in youth after-school programmes at the SDC, topics ranged from learning about the youths' family's migration history; positive self-talk; Filipino de-professionalization and community power; showcasing Filipino professionals; and accessing social services. Some facilitators used mindfulness/meditation tools, art, role-playing, video, and games. These programmes were developed in order to help Filipina/o/x youth make sense of their intersectional identities as well as to gain an understanding of their global migration experiences as newcomers through the L/CP. Filipina/o/x youth were able to safely engage with others about the impact of family separation and reunification, such as the reasons why their mothers are still stuck in low-paying jobs and why they barely see them. Along with this process in the workshops, such as positive self-talk, the youth were able to engage in how these global migration processes have impacted their transnational identities in Toronto urban schools. Thus, the SDC played a role in facilitating the youths' political agency through:

> *Processes of subjectification* – the processes which people become bearers of social structures. Processes of subjectification give the researchers access to ways of thinking and writing about categories such as a race, gender, sexuality….without reifying them and without divesting them of the historical relations of power through which they are produced. Analyses and narratives about who people are, and the lives they have lived, will always be incomplete if we cannot see the processes of social formation through which they became inaugurated as subjects.
>
> (Pascale, 2011, pp. 154–155)

One of the guidance counsellors who attended the after-school programmes at SDC explicated his privileged role as a white male while encouraging Filipina/o/x youth to challenge the forms of oppressions they face and observe on a daily basis. The youth engaged role-play activities and (re)enacted the difficulties of attaining jobs due to racialized, gendered, and classed oppressions. Interestingly, there were other newcomer and white Canadian youth who attended sessions. They shared that had it not been for the workshops they would not have known that many of the Filipina/o/x youth had been separated from their mothers for a long time. The purpose of the workshops was to assist the school staff in meeting the educational and social needs of the Filipina/o/x youth; to help build agency among the youth to become self-advocates; to help reduce isolation by connecting youth to community and social services; and to help youth understand the economic reasons for their parents' migration in order to help bridge relationship gaps due to family separation and reunification. Learning about their mothers' migration experience in through the lens of race, class, and gender facilitated engagement with the youth in embodied ways. Both NSC and SDC exemplified forms of transnational feminist praxis as they helped facilitated the political agency of Filipina/o/x youth, particularly in how to make sense of their identity and belonging in Toronto urban schools.

Throughout my fieldwork and participant-observation as co-performer, I learned firsthand that partnerships between Toronto urban schools and community organizations have the potential to create collaborative efforts by creating new spaces for Filipina/o/x youth to construct their political agency through after-school programmes. Nagar and Swarr (2010, p. 5) argue that political acts require a collaborative praxis, which can also apply to facilitating the political agency of Filipina mothers and their children specifically through:

> An intersectional set of understandings, tools, and practices that can: (a) attend racialized, classed, masculinized, and heteronormative logics and practices of globalization and capitalist patriarchies, and the multiple ways in which they (re)structure colonial and neocolonial relationships of domination and subordination;(b) grapple with the complex and contradictory ways in which these processes both inform and are shaped by a range of subjectivities and understandings of individual and collective agency; and (c) interweave critiques, actions, and self-reflexivity so as to resist a prior predictions of what might constitute feminist politics in a given place and time.

The workshops at the SDC and NSC attended to transnational feminist praxis in that the systemic oppression that influenced the youth's global migration were explored to facilitate their political agency. One particular white male student who frequently attended the workshops participated in one of the performances addressing the racial discrimination that Filipina/o/x newcomers face when looking for jobs. Interestingly, this particular white male student's role portrayed an exploitative employer who took advantage of the vulnerabilities of Filipina/o/x workers. A discussion followed and the guidance counsellor who attended these sessions pointed out his position as a white male who benefits from these forms oppressions and the ways in which these can be addressed. Filipina/o/x youth discussed how difficult it was for their parents, who were professionals in the Philippines, to obtain their respected professions in Canada. Sensing the feelings of heaviness and overwhelm of the newcomer students as well as the white male student, the facilitators at SDC engaged in "grounding" and "mindfulness" activities to help the students feel safe and acknowledge the impact of this stress on their bodies so they can further engage with the issues presented through this performance.

On November 30, 2016, I reflected upon the youth after-school programme at the SDC and NSC, especially upon the time I was part of a Filipino professional panel. The youth had asked what had led us to choose our careers. My answer was a vulnerable one as I hoped to embody collaborative transnational feminist praxis through my own firsthand experiences of racism, as "praxis can become a rich source of methodological and theoretical interventions and agendas that can begin the process of identifying and re/claiming…space" (Nagar & Swarr, 2010, p. 3). The sharing of the following experience speaks to the need to voice systemic oppression and its impact, as well as the need to create collaborative spaces for Filipina/o/x youth to make sense of their identity and belonging in Toronto urban schools:

> I was sitting at the panel with four other Filipina/o/x professionals, two were first generation and the other two were 1.5 generation as they came to Canada as young children. The panel was held in English as the

> audience was not all Filipina/o/x, though the majority were. The two first-generation Filipinos spoke in Tagalog, but myself and the 1.5 generation Filipinas spoke in English. I told them that the reason why I chose the careers that I did in social services and then in academia was because I was not welcomed in Canada while growing up, that my family experienced racism – it was right in our faces. The Filipina panelist also began to speak of her own experiences of racism, and started to tear up but held her tears back. This experience also influenced her to choose her career and to support her local community.

As Behar (1996) noted, ethnographers labour "through introspection. And then we go public again" (p. 9). Through sharing this story above, I was able to position myself as an insider/outsider in that my story of racism, migration, and discrimination impacted my identity and belonging in an urban school while growing up as a second-generation Filipina and co-performer. As an outsider, I was able to observe how my particular experience was situated in relation to others on the panel, as well as to the newcomer Filipina/o/x youth who have experienced various forms of systemic oppression. I chose to disclose vulnerabilities in relation to the purpose of the study and revealed, "keen understanding[s] of what aspects of the self are the most important filters through which one perceives the world, and more particularly, the topic being studied…a personal voice…can lead the reader…into the enormous sea of serious social issues" (Behar, 1996, pp. 13–14). The revelation may have helped the students to reflect upon their own positionalities in relation to the social concerns that exist inside and outside of Toronto urban schools.

In November 2016, I co-facilitate four workshops with Filipina/o/x parents at the SDC, and the main concerns that came out of these workshops were the strained relationships between left-behind children and the inability to repair these relationships years after reunification. Some of the parents were single mothers and some were married. All of the parents described the expectations they had of their children, but their actual school experiences did not reflect their expectations. Parents indicated that their children experienced bullying or lack of attendance in school and mentioned that guidance counsellors have suggested that the child get counselling and/or see a settlement worker for support. The parents reported that the school social workers would tell the youth to attend school because "it's the law".

One single mother shared that her son was caught for having drugs in his possession and that she did "not know how to parent". Zentgraf and Chinchilla (2012) maintained that due to long periods of separation and "a lack of parenting experience…create[s] challenges for parent-child reunion" (p. 357). The settlement worker and I listened to the mother as she explained that her son is a newcomer, and we asked her how the school is supporting the son with his adjustment to Canada. Answers included referring the students to school settlement workers, though not every school has a settlement worker to turn toward. Pratt (2010) argued that family separation and reunification through the L/CP has had a significant impact on the youth's educational experiences.

I reflected on this session afterwards, which was the second out of four sessions, recording this field note on November 13, 2016:

> We expect newcomer students to succeed just like that without really knowing what's going on. For social workers to tell student like this that "it's the law" to attend school doesn't really address the issue, I think. Individual counselling is a good idea, but I also think an understanding of the students' migration experiences is just as important. I don't think the mother or the son are to blame for the "lack of skills," but I think they do need to talk about how family separation and reunification have significantly impacted their relationship. I can imagine it's a very scary topic to even begin to talk about.

These workshops took place in the SDC site and guest speakers came to talk to parents about post-secondary options for themselves or for their child. One of the workshops included support from another worker at the SDC, and she talked about self-care for parents. I also provided referrals to social services that may address the needs of these families.

I also facilitated workshops on my own as an "insider" and community leader. From November to December 2016, I facilitated two social justice workshops at the SDC. The settlement worker and I planned the workshop together and we conducted a conversation circle or 'kwentuhan' (talk-story). Most of the students were Filipina/o/x in English Language Learners (ELLs) classes, but there were also newcomer students from Latin America, Europe, and the Middle East. We spoke about various topics such as gender & sexuality, migration, and Indigenous Nations. The settlement worker also spoke with about the importance of acknowledging Indigenous Peoples as the First Peoples on this land, making a connection of the land acknowledgement and Indigenous People at the beginning of the school day during the morning announcements. The students seemed to understand the concept of the community circle and shared where they had migrated from when it was their turn to speak. In a subsequent session, a student shared that as a newcomer, he did not feel safe in Toronto. He said that he did not fear physical harm, but he did feel the need to protect himself. The youth built on their conversations from the previous session and shared their experiences with sexuality, religion, spirituality, racism, sexism, and gender. One student from Latin America shared that people from his country of origin were physically punished those who belonged to the queer community and the students engaged in conversations around religion and "God", whom they held close to their hearts. We also engaged in an activity where students would learn about their social location and the purpose was to highlight who is privileged and/or marginalized.

Upon reflection of these two workshops, I wrote the following field note entry on November 28, 2016:

> Working with the youth and getting to know them better was the tool needed to help engage their embodied experiences of transnationalism. Providing concrete examples such as referring to the GSA in the school or explaining the purpose of acknowledging of Indigenous territories in the morning announcements facilitated the learning process. I think this is important for not only educators, but also social service workers who work with newcomers and youth. It is important not to impose academic and professional knowledge onto the youth yet it is crucial that educators/ social service providers engage in intimate ways so that students/youth have a relationship with the meanings of these words.

Overall, through these workshops, I learned the importance of embodying transnational feminist praxis through collaborative efforts to create space (Nagar & Swarr, 2010) for Filipina/o/x youth to engage in political agency as they make sense of their identity and belonging in Toronto urban schools. One of the ways in which these workshops engaged in transnational feminist praxis was through art, which stems from my belief "in the power of community-based art making to tap deep cultural histories, to engage peoples' hearts and minds through transformative process" (Barndt, 2010, p. 168). While the workshops were not explicitly "feminist", the facilitators did address the impact of family separation and reunification of mothers and children. Moreover, I was a participant-observer, in "feminist epistemological questions and methodological practices" (p. 168), as the SDC and the NSC and I collaborated in a way that engages in:

- Adopting an intersecting analysis of power;
- Honouring local and historically contingent practices, but within a context of globalizing processes;
- Focusing on situated knowledge and collaborative knowledge production;
- Promoting self-reflexivity;
- Using arts-based research methods to examine arts-based educational practices that challenge body/mind and reason/emotion dichotomies. (Barndt, 2010, p. 169).

The subsequent chapters will explore an intersectional analysis of power that honours the situated context of global migration through Canada's L/CP. This chapter highlighted my own reflexivity as a transnational feminist who engaged in arts-based research with Filipina/o/x youth. A key point in engaging in feminist epistemologies is collaborating with Filipina/o/x youth as a vulnerable observer (Behar, 1996) and co-performer (Madison, 2012) rather than a detached observer (Behar, 1996).

Embodying advocacy through performance ethnography

Challenging the enactment of the 'detached' researcher (Behar, 1996), feminist critical social theories frame how critical ethnography could look like (Madison, 2005). These frameworks also produce possibilities for dialogues and political interventions impacting local and global policies (Madison, 2012). Feminist critical social theories have been embedded in the study, particularly in its "intersecting analysis of power; honouring local and historically contingent practices, but within a context of globalizing processes [that focuses] on situated knowledges and collaborative knowledge production" (Barndt, 2010, p. 169).

This book draws upon "collaborative knowledge production" (Barndt, 2010, p. 169) through an engagement with "feminist epistemological questions and methodological practices" (Barndt, 2010, p. 168) as it illuminates the ways in which Filipina mothers mobilize their gendered vulnerabilities and its impact on Filipina/o/x youth. It sheds lights on the ways in which Filipina/o/x youth mobilize the traumas of family separation and reunification, particularly with their mothers. Finally, it looks at how school-community partnerships have facilitated the political agency of Filipina/o/x mothers and their children. Thus, these collaborative efforts shed light on the possibilities of implementing equitable educational policies and programmes beyond the school system, such as within im/migration and social services.

Drawing from Conquergood (2013), Johnson (2013) argues that the cultural performances of identity within performance ethnography produce spaces in which to speak back to structures of power, explicating how "macro-structures of political economy…impinge[s] on micro-textures of subjugated peoples' experience and how individuals caught within forbidden structures struggle for agency" (Johnson, 2013, p. 7). This book showcases how school-community partnerships engage in collaborative advocacy with Filipina mothers and their children and Filipina/o/x community leaders, producing deeper understanding(s) of mobilizing gendered vulnerabilities and the traumas of family separation and reunification through Canada's L/CP.

Vidaview Life Story Board: Going beyond 'fragmented stories'[6]

A key piece in engaging Filipina/o/x youth as co-performers and myself as witness was the utilization of visual and oral history methods through the Vidaview Life Story Board, a magnetic playboard typically used in community, clinical, and research settings. For the Filipina/o/x youths' individual interviews, the Vidaview Life Storyboard captures narratives, even complex ones (Chase et al., 2012). Such narratives include gathering important information with regards to circumstances, actions, cultural meanings, and significant relationships; addressing crises; reflecting on themes, personal stories, and feelings; identifying risks, resources, values, achievements, and important aspects of community (Chase et al, 2012). The Vidaview Life Storyboard also captures and maps events, changes, and acts across time (Chase et al., 2012), elicited deeper understandings of how Filipina/o/x youth mobilize their experiences of trauma, their mothers' gendered vulnerabilities, and how school-community partnerships facilitate their political agency.

Capturing memory and oral histories through the Vidaview Life Storyboard

Utilizing the Vidaview Life Story Board facilitated a visual and interactive cultural representation of the lives of Filipina/o/x youth as it provided options in how they wished to engage in memory and oral histories. Filipina/o/x youth engaged in the following ways: verbally (traditional interview style & storytelling), written format (poetry, writing a story, or writing words), and/or visually (drawing, using clay and/or magnets, as well as pictures) through three colour-coded 'zones' found on the Vidaview Life Storyboard (Figure 2.1). In the

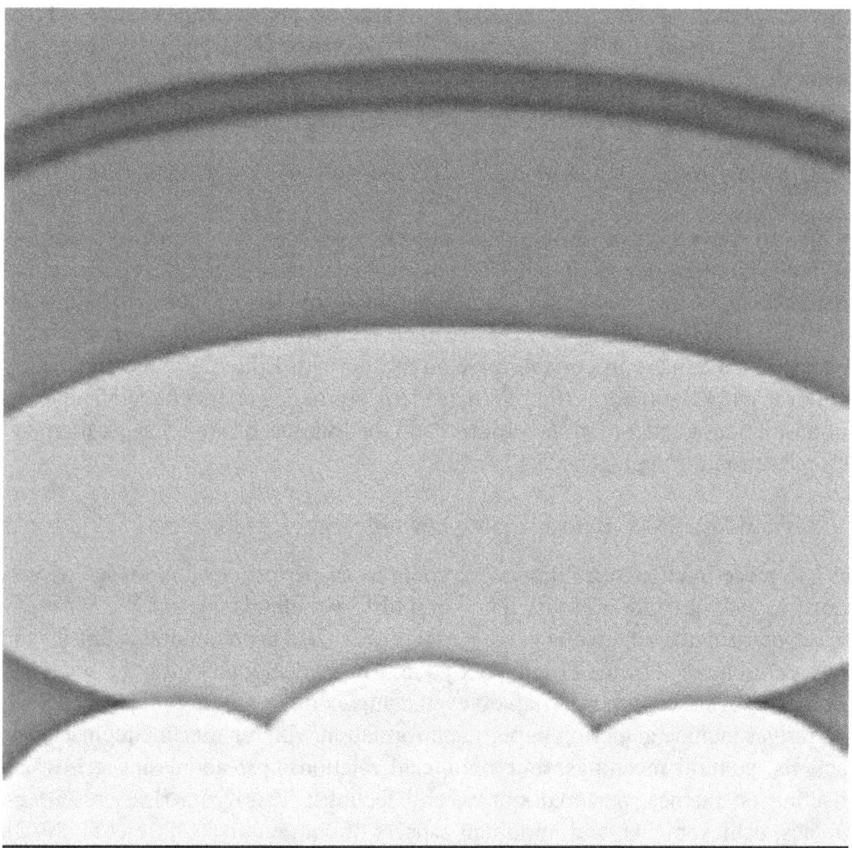

Figure 2.1 Image of Vidaview Life Story Board (Life Story Board, 2024)

Green Zone, the youth explored *Families and Close Relations*,[7] while in the *Yellow Zone,* they examined themes in relation to transnational *Representation[s] of Identity and Identity Constructions.*[8] Lastly, the youth discussed how they make meaning of *Community* in the *Blue Zone.*[9] Memory and oral histories refer to how particular subjectivities are remembered throughout historical moments through rich descriptions, narratives, and possibilities (Madison, 2012). The recollection of these particular stories and events are valid representations (Janesick, 2010) of Filipina/o/x youths' lives and transnational migration stories, where it is "both an act of memory and an inherently subjective account of the past" (Shopes, 2011, p. 452). Lastly, influential personal, psychological, collective, and social phenomena have construction of memory construction and of identities (Madison, 2012) among transnational Filipina/o/x youth.

Crystallization[10] and political advocacy through group art projects

A collective art piece depicting the transnational and embodied identities of Filipina/o/x youth represented their political agency as they reflected upon the themes of their individual interviews. The *Paper Quilt* (Taylor & Murphy, 2013), was a group art project that were based on the emergent themes from the Vidaview Life Storyboard and the specific guiding questions were: *What kinds of meaningful symbol(s), poems, stories, art remind you of your close relationships, particularly with your mother?* (Green Zone: Family/Close Relations)*; What kinds of symbols, poems, art, stories help you understand your identity as a Filipina/o/x person?* (Yellow Zone: Representation of Identity and Identity Constructions)*; What kinds of symbols, art, poems, stories, remind you of the meaningful relationships you have with Filipina/o/x community members?* (Blue Zone: Community). The Paper Quilt was then considered "a strategic means for political [and cultural] resistance...it is...a way to create...critical... dialogic space" (Finley, 2011, p. 446). Through this group art project, the youth mobilized the traumas of family separation and reunification through the L/CP by navigating its impact on the relationship with their mothers, their intersectional and transnational identities, and through their understandings of belonging within the Filipina/o/x community. This critical arts-based inquiry provided some "mechanisms and forms with which to see and hear each other's views on local socioeconomic systems, racial and cultural divides, and potential to develop common meeting spaces" (Finley, 2011, p. 435).

Filipina mothers, Filipina/o/x youth, and school–community partnerships

To elicit deeper understandings of the role school-community partnerships play in the political agency of Filipina/o/x youth and Filipina mothers, I investigated they have mobilized the experiences of transnational Filipina/o/x families as advocacy sites. This critical and performance ethnography consisted of twenty-two

Filipina/o/x youth within Toronto urban schools; nine Filipina/o/x community leaders who are involved school-community partnerships; and seven Filipina mothers who are former caregivers through the L/CP. Though the youth mostly had experienced family separation and reunification through the L/CP, a few youths did not have firsthand experiences of family separation and reunification through the L/CP. However, the latter were able to provide their perspectives as newcomers and as witnesses to the impact of family separation and reunification of their newly reunified peers. Community leaders were interviewed for their perspectives on their work with the Filipina/o/x community and through school-community partnerships. Filipina mothers and Filipina/o/x community leaders were interviewed for crystallization, a method that, "embraces, reveals, and even celebrates knowledge as inevitably situated, partial, constructed, multiple, and embodied" (Ellingson, 2011, p. 605). An integrated crystallization approach was utilized to provide a cultural representation that illuminates the complexities (Ellingson, 2011) of Filipina/o/x youths' transnational and intersectional identities. In the next chapter of this book, I explore how Filipina mothers mobilize the gendered vulnerabilities of the L/CP, which impacts the political agency of Filipina/o/x in Toronto urban schools.

Notes

1 Pseudonym.
2 Pseudonym.
3 Reverence and honour for the work being done (Dillard & Okapaloka, 2011).
4 According to Conquergood (2013), a co-performer is a researcher who embodies emotion in the field.
5 The four sources of cultural intuition are as follows: (1) personal experiences, (2) existing literature, (3) professional experiences, and (4) analytical research process.
6 In Pratt's (2010) interviews, the newly reunified youth engaged differently from second-generation Filipina/o/x youths and their Filipina mothers who eloquently described their transnational migration experiences and were able to articulate their activism in global injustices. Pratt describes the interviews with the reunified youth as "fragmented", but upon reflection recognized the youth had experienced multiple forms of trauma due to the L/CP and that she needed to look at their interviews through a different perspective.
7 See Chase et al. (2012) for more information.
8 Ibid.
9 Ibid.
10 See Ellingson (2011).

References

Anzaldúa, G. (1999). *Borderlands/La frontera* (2nd ed.). Aunt Lute Books.
Anthias, F. (2012). Intersectional what? Social divisions, intersectionality and levels of analysis. *Ethnicities*, *13*(1), 3–19.
Barndt, D. (2010). Remapping the Americas: A transnational engagement with creative tensions of community arts. In R. Nagar & A. L. Swarr, (Eds.), *Critical transnational feminist praxis* (York University ebrary Reader Version; pp. 166–191). Retrieved June 7, 2017, from http://ebookcentral.proquest.com.ezproxy.library.yorku.ca/lib/york/reader.action?docID=3407162&ppg=119

Behar, R. (1996). *The vulnerable observer: Anthropology that breaks your heart*. Beacon.

Bernal, D. D. (1998). Using a chicana feminist epistemology in educational research. *Harvard Educational Review*, *68*(4), 555–582.

Brah, A. (2003). Diaspora, border and transnational identities. In R. Lewis, & S. Mills (Eds.), *Feminist postcolonial theory: A reader* (pp. 613–634). Edinburgh University Press.

Chase, R.M., Medina, M.F. & Mignone, J. (2012). The life story board: A feasibility study of a visual interview tool for school counsellors. *Canadian Journal of Counselling and Psychotherapy/Revue canadienne de counseling et de psychothérapie 46*(3), 183–200.

Conquergood, L. D. (2013). In E.P Johnson (Ed.), *Cultural struggles: Performance, ethnography, praxis*. University of Michigan.

Dillard, C. B., & Okapaloka, C. (2011). The sacred and spiritual nature of endarkened transnational feminist praxis in qualitative research. In N. K. Denzin, & Y. S. Lincoln (Eds.), *SAGE handbook of qualitative research* (pp. 147–162). SAGE.

Ellingson, L. L. (2011). Analysis and representation across the continuum. In N. K. Denzin, & Y. S. Lincoln (Eds.), *SAGE handbook of qualitative research* (pp. 595–610). SAGE.

Erikson, F. (2011). A history of qualitative inquiry in social and educational research. In N. Denzin, & Y. Lincoln (Eds.), *The SAGE handbook of qualitative research* (pp. 43–60). SAGE.

Finley, S. (2011). Critical arts-based inquiry: The pedagogy and performance of a radical ethical aesthetic. In N. Denzin, & Y. Lincoln (Eds.), *The SAGE handbook of qualitative research* (pp. 435–450). SAGE.

González, M. C. (2000). The four seasons of ethnography: A creation-centred ontology for ethnography. *International Journal of Intercultural Relations*, *24*, 623–650.

Janesick, V. J. (2010). *Oral history for the qualitative researcher: Choreographing the story*. Guilford Press.

Johnson, E. P. (2013). Introduction: "Opening and interpreting lives. In E. P. Johnson (Ed.), *Cultural struggles: Performance, ethnography, praxis* (pp. 1–14). University of Michigan.

Life Story Board. (2024). *The Vidaview Life Story Board*™. https://dev.lifestoryboard.ca/.

Madison, D. S. (2012). *Critical ethnography: Method, ethics, and performance* (2nd ed.). Kindle Version]. Amazon.ca.

Mohanty, C. T. (2003). *Feminism without borders: Decolonizing theory, practicing solidarity*. Duke University Press.

Nagar, R., & Swarr, A. L. (2010). Critical Transnational Feminist Praxis. State University of New York Press.

Pascale, C. M. (2011). *Cartographies of knowledge: Exploring qualitative epistemologies*. SAGE.

Pierce, L. M. (2005). Not just my closet: Exposing familial, cultural, and imperial skeletons. In M. L. de Jesús (Ed.), *Pinay power: Peminist critical theory: Theorizing the Filipina/American experience* (pp. 31–44). Routledge.

Pratt, G. (2010). Listening for spaces of ordinariness: Filipino-Canadian youths' transnational lives. *Children's Geographies*, *8*(4), 343–352.

Scott, D., & Morrison, M. (2007). *Key ideas in educational research*. Continuum International.

Shopes, L. (2011). Oral History. In N. Denzin, & Y. Lincoln (Eds.), *The SAGE handbook of qualitative research* (pp. 451–466). SAGE.

Taylor, P., & Murphy, C. (2013). *Catch the fire: An art-full guide to unleashing the creative power of youth, adults and communities*. New Society Publishers.

Thomas, J. (1993). *Doing critical ethnography*. SAGE.

Vidaview Information Systems Ltd. (2012). Vidaview.ca

Zentgraf, K. M., & Chinchilla, N. S. (2012). Transnational family separation: A framework for analysis. *Journal of Ethnic and Migration Studies*, *38*(2), 345–366. https://doi.org/10.1080/1369183X.2011.646431

3 A mother's deep transnational love as resistance

> Right now, I am working at the factory…and I am a widow since 2008…I am a Registered Nurse back home but since I came here to Canada, I became a caregiver then a factor worker. In the Philippines, [I worked as a Registered Nurse] for 6.5 years…in Saudia Arabia…and then 3.5 years in Abu Dhabi. I came here in Canada in 2008 and after 3 months, my husband passed away…and I go back to the Philippines and after 6 months I am back as a caregiver and I completed my caregiver program and then I applied…as a factory worker.
>
> (Natalia[1], mother and former caregiver)

Introduction

In the previous chapter, I spoke about witnessing the political agency among Filipina mothers while exploring my positionality as a 'co-performer' (Madison, 2005) and 'vulnerable observer' (Behar, 1996) where I hold undeniable privilege as a scholar-activist and second-generation Filipina Canadian immigrant woman in relation to the participants. In this chapter, I excavate how Filipina mothers explore their political agency in relation to the gendered vulnerabilities of the L/CP, where "the Canadian government's decision to admit Filipino women under the L/CP as individual workers…[is] an arbitrary act of sovereign power that defines these women as less than citizens and temporarily strips them of their full personhood, including family relations" (Pratt, 2012, p. 71). I explore how Filipina mothers understand these 'sovereign' acts of degradation, particularly in how violates the ways in which they govern their own lives, wreaking potential havoc in their familial relations. Through these understandings, Filipina mothers mobilize the violent acts of the Canadian government through political agency.

These violent acts are not just local, but transnational and global. Through global migration, Filipina mothers have migrated to nation-states where the free-trade of products, labour, and goods are rampant (Sassen, 2008). The Philippine government encourages the labour exploitation of migrants through its participation in the global economy (Lutz, 2002) as an indebted country required to privatize their "public resources, to cut social spending, and to reorient their economies toward

DOI: 10.4324/9781003287469-3

export in order to earn foreign currency" (Jaggar, 2009, p. 40). These "global disciplining regime[s]" (Sassen, 2016, p. 209) have implemented Structural Adjustment Programs, lending money to countries in the Global South. However, these countries since the "economic crisis of the mid-1990s, the debt of poor countries in the South had grown from US $67 billion in 1980 to US $1.4 trillion in 1992" (p. 208). As of June 2023, the Philippines was in debt in the amount PHP (Philippine peso) 14.15 trillion (Bureau of the Treasury, 2023). On a transnational level, the Filipina/o/x diaspora, namely within the United States, Saudia Arabia, Singapore, and Japan, remitted $2.78 billion USD in 2023 (Bangko Sentral Ng Pilipinas, 2023). These global phenomena have had significant impact on the Philippines and has influenced Filipinas' mothers to migrate through the global domestic work industry, many times against their own volition to leave their families behind.

Context

Later throughout the chapter, I will introduce the Filipina mothers who have mobilized the gendered vulnerabilities of the global domestic work industry in Canada through political agency. Analysing the migration of Filipina mothers as a "response to a changing world economy" (Tyner, 1999, p. 61), this section examines the social, historical, and political context leading to the transnational migration of Filipina mothers, specifically through Canada's L/CP. Since the 1970s, the Philippine government has participated in the global economy through their own labour export policies to address the issues of unemployment and underemployment through remittances (Tyner, 1999). Consequently, migrant workers, such as Filipina caregivers, annually remit a part of their salaries to the Philippines government to repay foreign debt, with a portion given to their families (Friesen, 2011; Kessler & Rother, 2016; Pratt, 2012; Sassen, 2004). Foreign debt is also tied to the legacy of colonialism, which in turn, has impacted the transnational migration of Filipina mothers. The Philippines gained "independence" from Spain in 1898; Japan in 1943; and the United States in 1946 (Bankoff & Weekly, 2002). Arguably, since the 16th century, the beginning of Spanish colonialism, the Philippines has struggled "for freedom and a better life" (Constantino & Constantino, 1975, p. 81). Subsequently, American and Japanese colonialism nurtured, "a poverty-breeding society… [that suppressed] … any move for basic changes…[and] export crops predominated over produce to feed a grossly expanding population" (Constantino & Constantino, 1975, p. 394). These phenomena has had significant consequences on lives of Filipina mothers such as Courtney, Emilia, Evelyn, Natalia, Marcela, Tara, and Viviana[2], who left everything behind so that they could start anew on lands that in turn, have, and continue to exploit, their labour.

Filipina Mothers

A nurse from the Philippines and subsequently in Saudi Arabia and Abu Dhabi, Natalia migrated to Toronto, Ontario, Canada, through Canada's former Live-in/

Caregiver Program (L/CP), working from 2008-2015. Natalia's spouse passed away during the first few months of starting her work contract in 2008, so there was a gap in her required hours, but ultimately, she was able to obtain permanent residency for herself and her two children, Angelica and Brandon[3], as a single mother. Similar to many other reunified Filipina/o/x families, Natalia and her children were living with other low-waged Filipina caregivers in a one-bedroom rental unit. Prior migration, Natalia has been clear about her priorities: financially supporting her children so that they could pursue their hopes and dreams for success. She has shown deep care for her children, holding them accountable to their educational responsibilities, "I still know what's going on. [The school] also informs me about my [children's] lates and [absences]. This is how I monitor my kids" (Natalia, personal communication). Centring her children's futures is and was one of the main decisive factors in not pursuing her nursing career again in Canada. Furthermore, Natalia shared that she did not have Canadian work experience as a nurse and that her work as a caregiver would not count toward a nursing career.

While former Filipina caregivers like Natalia, Courtney, Emilia, Evelyn, Marcela, Tara, and Viviana held postsecondary degrees prior to migration, they had difficulties obtaining their previous professional careers in Canada, in part, due to the stigma of the racialized and gendered work of the L/CP (Banerjee et al., 2018), alongside financial constraints. Despite these stigmas, this chapter captures what Tuck (2009) describes as "desire-centred research", where marginalized communities are more than their "pain and brokenness" (p. 209). Furthermore, Tuck (2009) argues that:

> One alternative to damage-centred research is to craft our research to capture desire instead of damage. I submit that a desire-based framework is an antidote to damage-centred research. An antidote stops and counteracts the effects of a poison, and the poison I am referring to here is not supposed damage of Native communities, urban communities, or other disenfranchised communities but the frameworks that position these communities as damaged… desire-based research frameworks are concerns with understanding complexity, contradiction, and the self-determination of lived lives.
>
> (p. 416)

Like Tuck (2009), it is not my intention erase the gendered vulnerabilities that Filipina mothers experience or the "damage", however, this chapter highlights the desires that go beyond the damage. The "damage" of the L/CP centres the socio-historical context leading to global migration while the "desires" identify how future could look like in relation to the damage (Tuck, 2009). Thus, this chapter examines the ways in which Filipina mothers mobilize their own traumas of parenting far away from their children (Castañeda & Buck, 2011) and the gendered vulnerabilities (Jaggar, 2009) of the L/CP.

Natalia shared how difficult it was to be separated from Angelica and Brandon, her children:

> It was really hard [being away from my children], especially Brandon because he was 7 years old and 9 or before 10 years old for Angelica, so they were small when I was gone. It was hard because in the Philippines, the environment is really different, and they were there. So everyday, when I would chat with them, through a video call, I wanted to know what they ate, basically what they did the whole day, everyday, everyday, it was like that, especially with watching the news in the Philippines, so there's always crimes so I was really scared everyday, I called them everyday until the day they came to Canada, from 2008-2015 when they were in the Philippines…it was hard.
>
> (Natalia, personal communication)

While Filipina mothers appear to be locked into the domestic work industry due to feelings of love or indebtedness (Banerjee et al., 2018, p. 932), I argue that Filipina mothers have mobilized the gendered vulnerabilities of the L/CP through the love that they have for their children. Moreover, love is utilized as a tool and form of resistance to the exploitation and abuse within the L/CP. Below is a table representing the reasons for Filipina mothers' global migration through the L/CP as well as the mothers' current careers in Toronto, Ontario, Canada.

Table 3.1 showcases that the main reason for participating in the global domestic work industry was for economic reasons, highlighting the hopes and

Table 3.1 Demographic information about Filipina mothers

Pseudonym	*Mother/ father/ guardian/ parent*	*Single parent*	*Child is a participant of the study*	*Pseudonym and age of child*	*Reason for working in the L/CP*	*Current occupation*
Courtney	Mother	Yes	Yes	Chloe, 16	Economic	Unknown
Emilia	Mother	No	Yes	Eric, 18	Economic	Unknown
Evelyn	Mother	Yes	No	Children are aged 12, 14, 16	Economic	Unknown
Natalia	Mother	Yes	Yes	Angelica, 17	Economic	Factory worker
Marcela	Mother	Yes	No	Children aged 6 & 7	Economic	Caregiver (Children)
Tara	Mother	No	Yes	Alicia, 18	Economic	Unknown
Viviana	Mother	No	No	Children aged 11 & 12	Economic	Personal Support Worker (full-time); Caretaker (part-time)

dreams for their children's futures in Canada. This table illuminates that many of the mothers still largely remain in low-wage jobs, even after obtaining permanent residency for themselves and their children.

Strategic mobilizing of the gendered vulnerabilities[4] of the L/CP

I argue that Filipina mothers like Natalia mobilize the gendered vulnerabilities (Jaggar, 2009) of the L/CP that render them invisible in 'global cities' (Sassen, 2008) through political agency. 'Global cities' are a microcosm of the 'global economy' as "the consumption practices of high-income professionals…generate a demand for low-wage workers…for…nannies at home" (Sassen, 2008, p. 459). 'Nannies', such as Filipina mothers, experience the feminization of labour within the global domestic work industry, like L/CP, "where millions of women cross borders…to seek employment" (Jaggar, 2009, p. 41). These "low-wage domestic workers are in fact strategic infrastructure maintenance workers" (Sassen, 2008, p. 488) that "ease the entrance of women into the paid labor market force but also assist in the economic growth of receiving countries" (Parreñas, 2004, p. 107), such as settler colonial nation-states like Canada. Gendered vulnerabilities such as "frequently receiv[ing] low pay and suffer[ing] long hours, high pressure, employment insecurity, and sexual harassment [and violence]" (Jaggar, 2009, p. 35), are reproduced due to the scarcity of jobs and reliance on remittances in their home countries (Jaggar, 2009).

Viviana[5] is a client of *Services for a Diverse Community* (SDC)[6] and a mother who reunified with her family through the L/CP. She describes her experience with continually sending remittances back to the Philippines, "The money here is much [more] helpful to send back home. I still have my parents who [are still] waiting for help and I still have siblings who [go] to school." Despite having completed the L/CP and obtaining permanent residency for her family, Viviana continually remits back to her family in the Philippines while also financially supporting her two children ages 11 and 12 here in Canada. Poor countries, such as the Philippines, rely on migrant workers like Natalia and Viviana to remit their low-waged earnings to help them get out of foreign debt (Jaggar, 2009).

Nevertheless, Filipina mothers' political agency lies in their "ongoing and situated negotiation of self-naming and being named by others that relies on visible and non-visible markers of difference and is implicated in power relations" (Coloma, 2008, p. 20). The political agency among Filipina mothers comprises "specific political projects aimed at constructing belonging in particular ways to particular collectivities that are, at the same time, themselves being constructed by these projects in a very particular way" (p. 197). Political agency plays a crucial role in mobilizing the gendered vulnerabilities of Filipina mothers. I argue that political agency requires a shift from notion 'victimhood' to the empowerment of migrant domestic workers (Briones, 2009).

While rendered invisible in global cities (Sassen, 2008), Tungohan (2012; 2017; 2023) maintains that despite lacking formal Canadian citizenship, Filipina caregivers have been the centre of political activism and advocacy. Through political agency, I posit that Filipina mothers have resisted the gendered vulnerabilities of the L/CP through everyday resistances (Chee, 2023; Le, 2022; Roces, 2021), namely through their hopes and dreams for their children's socio-economic futures.

Hopes and Dreams: Micro forms of Resistance

Drawing from Chee's (2023) understanding of 'counter-conduct', I look at the ways in which Filipina mothers transform themselves as oppressed objects to subjects "capable of "doing politics", albeit in…[an] informal, everyday sense" (p. 594). As subjects continually reclaiming their dignity and self-worth through rest, leisure, and care, Filipina mothers "resist economic exploitation" (Chee, 2023, p. 595). The main catalyst for this form of resistance are they hopes and dream they have for the futures of their children. Following Tuck's (2009) 'desire-centred' framework, I posit that Filipina mothers mobilize the gendered vulnerabilities of the L/CP through the hopes and dreams that they have throughout the global migration process. The 'desire-centred' framework links to Tuck and Yang's (2014) 'Theory of Change', which is "about how a situation can be adjusted, corrected, or improved" (p. 13). Through 'counter-conduct' (Chee, 2023), Filipina mothers embody the 'Theory of Change' (2014), resisting the structures of local and global heteropatriarchy through individual and collective agency (Nagar & Swarr, 2010). Filipina mothers have remained steadfast, holding on to the hopes and dreams for themselves and their children, "regardless of the economic challenges that they themselves faced during and after the L/CP, most saw their future in Canada and felt that coming to the country was "worth it" (Tungohan et al., 2015, p. 87).

Tungohan (2023) describes 'care activism' as a form of resistance among Filipina caregivers:

> Migrant caregiver activists use their embodied knowledge of oppressive structures and institutions to disrupt the status quo. The framework of care activism…draws attention to covert sites of resistance…a primary intervention…[that showcase] sites of resistance that are often sidelined in academic analyses in favour of research on public protest actions that are driven by the need to change policies and shift discourses…it also involves everyday resistances.
>
> (p. 5)

While this chapter acknowledges the importance of shifting political discourses and involving Filipina migrant workers in the frontlines of protests, it focuses on the everyday resistances, specifically their hopes and dreams for their children as a form of resistance.

Evelyn[7] is a former caregiver and a client of the SDC. A single parent who was an educator in the Philippines, Evelyn indicated that she works full- time in a low-income position and part-time at a cleaning job. She shared that she wanted her sons to value education, because if they did not, they would become "like her":

Evelyn:	Sometimes I'm bringing them in my job…[My cleaning job] because I have my part-time in the office, like cleaning in the office.
Researcher:	You have two jobs?
Evelyn:	Yes, I have two jobs.
Researcher:	Wow!
Evelyn:	Even for an hour, I am bringing them. And I am showing them if you don't study, this is your world. This is how hard your work is, so if you study and you pick the right course for you, you study well, you have a nice job, and you're not going to be like me.
Researcher:	So you work full-time as a PSW (Personal Support Worker) and then part-time cleaning?
Evelyn:	PSW, full-time, and cleaning, part-time.

The dialogue I had with Evelyn contains many layers. First, it is evident that Evelyn still faces the residual effects of the gendered vulnerabilities within the global domestic work industry (Jaggar, 2009), working in a low-paying job even after obtaining permanent residency for herself and her family through the completion of the L/CP. I also argue that Evelyn's conversation with her children is a 'counter-conduct' act[8] that challenges the effects of these particular gendered vulnerabilities through a reclamation of dignity and self-worth (Chee, 2023) for herself *and* her children. Thus, Evelyn mobilizes the gendered vulnerabilities of a her low-wage job as she holds on to hopes and dreams for her children's futures.

In Collin's (2000) 'Toward a Politics of Empowerment', "Black diasporic feminisms…must "never stop questioning" social injustices" (p. 273). In Evelyn's situation above, she brings her children to her workplace so that they do not become "like her". Through action, and not so much with words, she is questioning the injustices of her work and wants to protect her children from the structural violence of gendered and racialized vulnerabilities as marginalized community members in Canadian society. I argue that Evelyn's actions are acts of resistance that move toward empowerment of herself and her children, where she centres the futures hopes and dreams for her children, the very reason why she had engaged in transnational migration and battled with gendered vulnerabilities. Collins (2019) argues that acts of empowerment require "transforming unjust social institutions that African-Americans encounter from one generation to the next" (p. 273).

Within the Filipina/o/x context, Evelyn engages in the politics of empowerment by illuminating the gendered vulnerabilities of transnational migration, attempting to change the pattern for her children, the future generation. Furthermore, through her 'counter-conduct' (Chee, 2023), she continually questions the intergenerational forms of social injustice and moves toward a politics of empowerment (Collins, 2000; 2019). This move of resistance mobilizes the representation of Filipina mothers as passive victims of the L/CP into that of political agency, where, despite their gendered vulnerabilities, they exhibit forms of advocacy and belonging (Tungohan, 2012; 2017; 2023). Ultimately, Filipina mothers mobilize their gendered vulnerabilities to resist exclusion (Antonsich, 2010) for themselves and their children.

> I am a single mother because my husband died…[and]…I needed the money when my kids came. So after being a caregiver, I got an open permit, I applied to the factory…Unfortunately, since I am always working at the factory, I never had the time to attend their parent's meeting at school. I know that they want me to show up but I just can't because I would rather miss the meeting than lose the money that we could use for our daily needs.
>
> (Natalia, personal interview)

Filipina mothers have been accused of neglecting the needs of their children, particularly through abandoning them through the L/CP (Tungohan, 2013). However, they have resisted these perspectives through, "constant surveillance and contact with their children, allowing them to meet societal expectations concerning maternal care" (Tungohan, 2013, p. 47). Many of the Filipina mothers I spoke with regarding their children's educational success also challenged this dominant narrative of 'neglect'. For instance, Natalia states, that while she cannot attend meeting as the sole financial provider, she keeps updated with the school through regular communication with Brandon's and Angelica's educators and holds them accountable to their respective tasks. For instance, other Filipina mothers and former caregivers shared that their hopes and dreams for their children's futures had been particularly salient within educational success. Courtney[9], imparted to her daughter, Chloe[10], 16, values in achieving her dreams through hard work. Tara[11] consistently assesses her daughter, Alicia[12]'s, 18, overall well-being:

> As a mother, my hopes, expectations, and dreams for my children are just simple. I just [want] them to finish their university and find a good job and be stable so that they can stand on their own when they're already on their own. [Alicia] is not completely adjusted yet, but she improved a lot especially on her study habits and attitude. She is more mature now when it comes to managing her time and making decisions especially on what courses to take and what school to choose for…her university.

Thus, these everyday resistances and 'counter-conduct' acts (Chee, 2023) provide space for social transformation (Le, 2022) that may lead to individual acts of resistance to mezzo forms of contestation "to a more organized public expression of defiance" (Pande, 2012, p. 384). These mezzo level acts of resistance are, "strategic acts that cannot be classified as either private and individual or as organized collective action" (Pande, 2012, p. 368), where school-community partnerships engage in community level interventions.

Mezzo forms of resistance: School-community partnership interventions

> As a caregiver, there are no benefits and for the caregivers, it's better that our salaries are the same, you know cause there are employers that are so stingy and if you go there, your salary will be low…yes that's what's wrong with the Caregiver Program, there's no benefits…I don't know why it takes so long for others to get benefits, it's hard when you don't have benefits, especially if your family is here, and if something happens, what'll happen next? What are you going to do? Also, some of my caregiver friends who applied for permanent residency also spent so much money one medical after another, they even spent up to $10, 000 for their family members.
>
> (Natalia, family interview)

Here, Natalia engages in 'counter-conduct' acts that challenge the exploitation, precarity, and gendered vulnerabilities of the L/CP impacting the community of Filipina caregivers. Mezzo-level resistances move from individual acts to "a more organized public expression of defiance. The mezzo-level of resistive acts and the alliances formed potentially provide a basis for more radical resistance to domination" (Pande, 2012, p. 384). Mezzo forms of resistance occur in unexpected places & spaces, such as through school-community partnerships, which mainly consisted of Filipina/o/x community leaders working within the school system. These school-community partnerships were mainly located in low-income urban neighbourhoods, and it is through school-community partnerships that Filipina mothers have shifted from micro to mezzo levels of resistance where they can connect with community leaders and other Filipina mothers who have been and are going through similar and unique experiences of family separation and reunification through the L/CP.

Accessing parenting workshops and individualized support through school-community partnerships, Filipina mothers can resist stereotypes of victimhood and mobilize their gendered vulnerabilities through political agency. Through community support, Francisco-Menchavez (2018) argues that Filipina migrant workers:

> worked to create a community that was an extension of acts of care and service they performed for their own transnational families. Migrant

> women built these networks of care using Filipino cultural traditions of fictive kinship and bayanihan (camaraderie) because of the marginalization and other difficult circumstances they experienced.
>
> (p. 101)

Through school-community partnerships, Filipina mothers have collectively mobilized the gendered vulnerabilities of the L/CP, contesting the forms of power (Cho et al., 2013) that continually reproduce their marginalization. Furthermore, Francisco-Menchavez (2018) argues that "once a domestic worker shares a negative work experience, others are then invited to share…this process can encourage migrants to share their struggles but also engage in a collective process to identify strategies for coping and resisting" (p. 159). This chapter looks at the ways in which Filipina/o/x community leaders have been part of these resistance process.

Sherry[13], a Filipina community leader, shared that leaders and students alike were going through their own identity and belonging processes, particularly Filipina/o/x youth who have experienced family separation and reunification through the L/CP. Sherry, trained as a social worker, possesses thorough understanding of anti-oppressive and decolonization processes, particularly within the context of settler colonialism in Canada and global migration. A second-generation Filipina Canadian like myself, Sherry explores the possibilities of facilitating community work at the mezzo level in relation to her own positionality:

> To acknowledge that…we are still learning more about ourselves in this context and we by learning with them and feeling some of the things that they're doing, we then get to learn deeper about ourselves…it's good that more of these opportunities to learn with other cultures is happening, but how do we facilitate? What [do Filipina mothers and their children] understand about…coming to Canada as [im/migrants], and how do we support developing that identity [with] them because that's a hard one, and that goes again to that piece of being reflected in who is your support system, in your communities, and in your education system, because…you don't have people to reflect back to you something strong and positive. And how are you supposed to feel about yourself? How are you supposed to know you can move forward and achieve things when that's not being reflected to you? So I think that plays hand in hand.
>
> (Sherry, individual interview)

Sherry provides thought-provoking dialogue that needs unpacking, particularly in relation to Filipina mothers' engagement in mezzo-level community resistance and the positionality of Filipina/o/x community leaders providing service and programming to Filipina mothers and their children. In terms of positionality, Sherry points out that as intergenerational Filipina/o/x community leaders, we need to acknowledge our role in relation to Filipina mothers and their children. I acknowledge the privilege and power that I have as an academic researcher who holds Canadian Citizenship as this impacts the levels of trust and the ethic of care when engaging in school-community partnerships with transnational families. As co-performers and witnesses[14], community leaders such as Sherry and myself are learning our intersectional identities alongside Filipina mothers and their children, as well as our own support systems within school-community partnerships. The use of *Bayanihan* (Francisco-Menchavez, 2018) is an important form of transnational feminist praxis that uses culturally-relevant values to engage in community organizing and resistance on a mezzo level. Through school-community partnerships Filipina mothers have strengthened "their ties with one another even in the face of exploitation and precariousness" (Francisco-Menchavez, 2018, p. 101). Thus, Filipina mothers have mobilized their gendered vulnerabilities due to Bayanihan within school-community partnerships, continually holding on to the hopes and dreams that they have for their children's futures.

In addition to bayanihan, de Guia (2014) draws from Enriquez's (1973; 1992) *kapwa* Filipino psychology, a concept that is relevant in mezzo levels of resistance among Filipina mothers. *Kapwa* refers to:

> *Kapwa,* the central value of personhood, builds a bridge between the innermost core of one person to anyone outside – including total strangers… The tagalog "kapwa" is widely used when addressing another with the intention of establishing a connection…such notion of mutual Self greatly contrasts the Western interpretation, where the self is individual – something that excludes others and cannot be shared…implicit in in such inclusiveness, however, is the moral obligation to treat one another as equals. Enriquez, therefore, speaks of "humanness as its highest level", where a person's ethic/behavio[u]r counts, not [their] external trappings.
>
> (p. 140)

Kapwa then, becomes an important aspect in conceptualizing resistance with a transnational context, specifically in global cities and urban educational spaces such as Toronto, Canada. Through *pakiramdam,* the "aptitude of putting one in the other's shoes or looking at things from many different angles" (de Guia, 2014, p. 141), Filipina mothers engage in empathy and looking at different forms of knowledges and truths that they encounter in their migration trajectories. Through shared connections, specifically with other Filipina caregivers' ancestral beliefs such as "*kandahang-loob* – shared nobility. This concept acts as an ethic measure that helps people to streamline their feelings according to… love…Enriquez assigns this value to the core of Filipino personhood…toward genuine acts of generosity; towards a nurturing…in genuine…empathy" (de Guia, 2013, p. 141).

Resistance toward oppressive regimes has been deeply engrained with Filipino socio-political history in fact, "the Filipino resistance was not easily crushed throughout many centuries of occupation, points to a psychology that is propelled by values of valor" (de Guia, 2013, p. 141). There are three forms of resistance that Filipinos had confronted their oppressors: *bahala-na; lakas ng loob; pakikibaka. Bahala-na* means "Leave things up to God!", however, scholars in the U.S. have misunderstood to mean "fatalism" (de Guia, 2013, p. 142). de Guia (2013) draws from Lagmay's (1977) interpretation of *bahala-na:*

> As a value, he suggests, *bahala-na* stands for a unique resolve that operated in uncertain and uncharted situation. It implied risk-taking in the face of possible failure and accepting the very nature of things (including one's own limitations) while pushing onwards to find a creative twist that would solve a problem...The creative approach of *bahala-na* allows Filipinos to keep on trying to improve their lot while learning from each turn along the way. Such an approach builds confidence as it gives a person a chance to accrue experiences of how to master at kids of difficulties effectively... such a norm-defiant position is in itself subversive."
>
> (de Guia, 2013, p. 142)

Filipina mothers are thus able to resist the gendered vulnerabilities of the L/CP through *bahala-na* through taking creative ways to connect with community and learn from one another through *lakas ng loob,* feelings of bravery and fearlessness. Drawing from Enriquez, de Guia (2013) indicates that *lakas ng loob* is '"the inner resources for change'...and also awakens the goodness in others" (p. 143). Community organizing throughout Philippine history reflects the contemporary *lakas ng loob* that Filipina mother engage in with school-community partnerships and other Filipina mothers, "for centuries, it upheld the peasants' fighting spirit and ideals of insubordination...this type of ardor has remained incomprehensible to the Western eye" (p. 143). Lastly, the third value of resistance is through *pakikibaka,* which "can facilitate a level of fusion among even most diverse communities, rousing all people into a concerted action...in one arbitrary moment of revolution, they all assert their strength and collectively fight" (de Guia, 2013, p. 93). Thus, synthesizing these three Filipino values of resistance provides space for Filipina mothers, Filipina/o/x youth, and school-community partnerships to engage in *pakikibaka,* despite the power relations that are embedded in urban educational systems in global cities.

Macro forms of resistance, School-Community partnerships & political projects

School-community partnerships play a significant role in macro levels of intervention, particularly in how they facilitate Filipina mothers' resistance against dominant forces of globalization, capitalism, imperialism, and heteropatriarchal norms. Natalia, like many Filipina mothers, demonstrate these forms of resistance through the hopes and dreams for their children:

> My eldest child [Angelica] [sees] how hard life in Canada is which is why she is motivated to study well and have a good job. Despite…having 2 jobs, she still manages to do good at school. Just recently, she received 3 academic awards for being [an] outstanding student… She also received an honour role award. My son look[s] up to her even though he doesn't admit it…now, he is more eager to do well in school since he want to be like [his] ate [his older sister]. This is the main reason [for] letting your kids know how tough life is. It motivates them to do better.
>
> (Natalia, individual interview)

Through school-community partnerships, Natalia demonstrates how she has mobilized the gendered vulnerabilities of the L/CP through motivating her children. While holding onto the hopes and dreams she has for her children, Natalia is upfront about the difficulties for marginalized communities in Canada such as achieving their careers and upward mobility (Kelly, 2014).

In addition to school-community partnerships facilitating the political agency of Filipina mothers and their children, further macro-level interventions are necessary. As privileged spaces embedded in power relations, Anyon (2013) proposes the need for educational systems to economically support marginalized communities, particularly in low-income neighbourhoods. As Filipina mothers and their children, migrate to low-income neighbourhoods in Toronto, Ontario, Canada, school-community partnerships need to consider the means to economically support low-income families (Anyon, 2013), particularly single income households. With economic resources and support through school-community partnerships, Filipina mothers and their children can work toward mobilizing the gendered vulnerabilities of the L/CP and achieving their hopes and dreams for the future.

School-community partnerships may facilitate collaborative work by connecting Filipina mothers and their children to key organizations and activist groups where, "resistance…can be waged by the oppressed, by advocates and sympathizers…As they engage in collective resistance, [school-community partnerships can] form movement organizations that become expressions of their collective identity and which can help sustain their struggle" (Lindio-McGovern, 2007, p. 16). Furthermore, school-community partnerships may help heal broken relationships from a micro to macro level:

> A symbolic connection to the familiar, to 'home,' to the land from which they were torn. …the relationships nurtured therein thus serve as strategic sites of empowerment, belonging, and healing [that allow] them to thrive in supportive environments surrounded by other Filipinos who have similarly coped with the pain and frustration associated with long-term

> family separation. Their involvement enabled them to build lasting bonds of friendship with other Filipino migrant families but most importantly, nurtured possibilities of post-reunification reconciliation between [Filipina mothers and their children.]
>
> (de Leon, 2014, p. 9)

Identifying sites of empowerment are important within 'desire-centred research' (Tuck, 2009) as Filipina/o/x youth and their mothers relate to one another with one commonality: being displaced from 'home'. In terms of home, the Philippines had been considered one of the youths' transnational homes. As de Leon (2014) identified above, long term separation involves feelings of pain and frustration that can exacerbate ruptured familial relationships, particularly when newly reunified children left their loved ones behind in the Philippines (Pratt, 2012; Ticar, 2017). However, this chapter highlights how healing through community (de Leon, 2014) can help connect Filipina mothers and their children as well as Filipina/o/x community leaders through school-community partnerships.

These macro forms of intervention through school-community partnerships need to consider transnational care activism:

> Transnational engagements are crucial to understanding how care activism as a framework for migrant organizing goes beyond the national. This is especially the case when considering how migrant care workers have transnational lives in that they live in Canada but are supporting families in other parts of the world...by being part of these transnational spaces, migrant care workers activists contest the neoliberal economic project that sending and receiving states are complicit in, pointing to how it is these economic structures that facilitate their labour migration and their separation from their families.
>
> (Tungohan, 2023, p. 105)

Evelyn, while already reunited with her spouse and children, still sends remittances back to the Philippines to support her parents and siblings, on top of providing for her family here in Canada, thus, exemplifying how transnational care exists beyond geographical location. Additionally, she recognizes that her remittances require labour exploitation through the L/CP as well as through her two low-paying jobs. The next section of this chapter explores the possibilities of how which transnational care activism and praxis could look like within school-community partnerships.

School-community partnerships and transnational feminist praxis

Transnational feminism(s) provides a framework in understanding how Filipina mothers *mobilize* the structures of gendered vulnerabilities, moving away from centring the "damage" (Tuck, 2009) and focusing their children's future hopes and dreams. Despite the structural violence embedded within the L/CP, Filipina mothers engage in political agency by demonstrating that their own lives matter (Tungohan, 2012). Transnational feminisms are theoretical and practical interventions that centre the "mutually constituting relations of heteropatriarchal, capitalist, racial, and colonial authority, as well as the possibilities of transformative change that arise from feminist practices of resurgence and resistance oriented towards coalitions across borders" (Dhamoon, 2015, p. 27). This chapter highlights how Filipina mothers mobilize the gendered vulnerabilities of the L/CP that is mutually constituted upon these forms of oppression. Since the colonization of the Philippines has impacted the global migration decisions of Filipina mothers, transnational feminism has an anti-colonial approach to nation-states such as Canada, where the "problem is the imposition of colonial heteropatriarchal structures" (Dhamoon, 2015, p. 27). Transnational feminism attempts to address the continuum of colonialism through anti-colonial praxes that are not necessarily limited to movement between nation-states, but also "to the battleground of the settler-colonial nation-state and Indigenous nationhood in the wider global context of white supremacy and capitalist flows of migration and labour" (Dhamoon, 2015, p. 27).

Additionally, transnational feminisms "must make links between a critique of transnational corporations that exploitatively extract natural resources on traditional Indigenous territories with state support, global markets that exploit Third World women's labour for the benefit of the West, and Indigenous and women of colour organizing against these modalities of gendered colonialisms and racisms, some of which are grounded in Indigenous conceptions of nationhood" (Dhamoon, 2015, p. 28). In terms of decolonization, transnationalism feminism can be conceptualized "beyond the scope of the state and through a centre-to-centre dynamic of relationality" (Dhamoon, 2015, p. 28).

School-community partnerships have engaged in these forms of transnational feminisms with their work with Filipina/o/x parents, particularly Filipina mothers who have experienced family separation and reunification through the L/CP. Many of the Filipina mothers who attended parenting workshops stated that they struggled in their relationship with their children and that "did not know how to parent". These forms of praxes provided deeper understanding(s) to among the youth their mothers had their best interest at heart when making the decision to "leave". The parenting programs helped Filipina mothers understanding the impact of the L/CP on their children that reinforced that global migration through the L/CP was "worth it" (Tungohan et al., 2015, p. 87).

School-community partnerships are also the site in which to "build alliances by learning and actively engaging with multiple struggles across hegemonic borders of gender, sexuality and desire, race, coloniality, labour, dis/ability, the movement of bodies, capital, territory, and land" (Dhamoon, 2015, p. 34). These partnerships provide transnational and transformative spaces for Filipina/o/x youth to understand these social constructions through art and kuwentuhans (talk-story) in relation to the gendered vulnerabilities of their mothers' global migration experiences through the L/CP. Thus, school-community partnerships have also provided spaces of possibility to engage in transnational feminist praxis, which may be understood as:

> Intersectional set of understandings, tools, and practices that can: a) attend to racialized, classed, masculinized, and heteronormative logics and practices of globalization and capitalist patriarchies, and the multiple ways in which they (re) structure colonial and neocolonial relations of domination and subordination; (b) grapple with the complex and contradictory ways in which these processes both inform and are shaped by a range of subjectivities and understandings of individual and collective agency; and (c) interweave critiques, actions, and self-reflexivity so as to resist a priori predictions of what might constitute feminist politics in a given place and time."
>
> (Nagar & Swarr, 2010, p. 5)

School-community partnerships have engaged with Filipina mothers and their children through their understanding of transnational feminist praxis, specifically in imparting their knowledge(s) of the power relations and gendered vulnerabilities of the global domestic work industry, particularly, the impact of colonial histories on contemporary global migration experiences through the L/CP. School-community partnerships have facilitated the agency of Filipina mothers and their children by providing these transnational feminist spaces within Toronto urban schools.

School-community partnerships provide possibilities for understanding the gendered vulnerabilities of Filipina caregivers through the global domestic work industry, and specifically, the former Live-in/Caregiver Program, as this was the program that all of the Filipina mothers had completed. These partnerships provided workshops for parents to navigate the difficulties and processes of family separation through the L/CP, and in terms of after school programming, Filipina/o/x youth learned about the socio-historical trajectories of global migration through the L/CP and about economic reasons for their mothers' im/migration. School-community partnerships engaged in art as a tool to understand the macro reasons for global migration and the impact on the micro and mezzo levels impacting their lived experiences. One student demonstrated his understandings of his mother's global migration experience through the L/CP through his drawings, which include an image of broken chains and money "break the chains of poverty" for economic reasons. Thus, school-community partnerships facilitate the political agency of Filipina mothers and the traumas of family separation and reunification by eliciting understandings of the macro influences impacting the lived experiences of Filipina mothers and their children through transnational feminism.

Conclusion

Throughout this chapter, I have highlighted the various ways in which Filipina mothers have engaged in individual and collective agency in relation to the gendered vulnerabilities embedded within the global domestic work industry, specifically through Canada's Live-in/Caregiver Program. The individual and collective hopes and dreams for their children's futures are the forms of resistance Filipina mothers engage in and where they demonstrate political agency.

School-community partnerships engage in transnational feminist praxis (Nagar & Swarr, 2010), offering key understandings in how to engage in transnational community organizing within a situated context. While Filipina mothers have experienced of gendered vulnerabilities and the traumas of family separation and reunification, this chapter also highlights how Filipina mothers engage in political agency. School-community partnerships have also provided spatial possibilities of engagement in *bayanihan* (Francisco-Menchavez, 2018) and other Filipina/o/x cultural values through the knowledge and understandings of Filipina/o/x community leaders. In subsequent chapters, I discuss in further detail the role of school-community partnerships in decolonizing education, Indigenous-settler relations, and critical social justice. Additionally, I examine how they address the traumas that youth face due to family separation and reunification through the global domestic work industry.

Notes

1 Pseudonym.
2 Pseudonyms.
3 Angelica and Brandon are pseudonyms. Angelica and Brandon were both in their early 20s in February 2022, during the time of the interview for my postdoctoral study.
4 Jaggar, 2009. (Is gendered vulnerabilities explained anywhere)?
5 Pseudonym.
6 Pseudonym.
7 Pseudonym.
8 See Chee (2023).
9 Pseudonym.
10 Pseudonym.
11 Pseudonym.
12 Pseudonym.
13 Pseudonym.
14 See Madison (2012).

References

Antonsich, M. (2010). Searching for belonging: An analytical framework. *Geography Compass*, *4*(6), 644–659.

Anyon, J. A. (2013). Political economy of race, urban education, and educational policy. In C. McCarthy, W. Crichlow, G. Dimitriadis, & N. Dolby (Eds.), *Race, Identity, and Representation in Education*, (2nd ed.) (pp. 369–378).

Banerjee, R., Kelly, P., Tungohan, E., Cleto, P., de Leon, C., Garcia, M., Luciano, M., Palmaria, C., & Sorio, C. (2018). From "Migrant" to "Citizen": Labor Market Integration of Former Live-In Caregivers In Canada. *ILR Review*, *71*(4), 908–936. https://doi.org/10.1177/0019793918758301

Bangko Sentral Ng Pilipinas. *Personal Remittances Reach US$2.8 Billion in May 2023; YTD Growth at 3.1 Percent.* (2023). Retrieved from: https://www.bsp.gov.ph/SitePages/MediaAndResearch/MediaDisp.aspx?ItemId=6793

Bankoff, G., & Weekley, K. (2002). *Post-colonial National Identity in the Philippines: Celebrating the Centennial of Independence*. Aldershot, England; Burlington, VT: Ashgate.

Behar, R. (1996). *The Vulnerable Observer: Anthropology that Breaks your Heart*. Boston: Beacon.

Briones, L. (2009). *Empowering Migrant Women: Why Agency and Rights are not Enough* (1st ed.). Routledge. https://doi.org/10.4324/9781315579399

CastañedaBuck2011). Remittances, transnational parenting, and the children left behind: Economic and psychological implications. *The Latin Americanist*, *55*, 85–110.

Bureau of the Treasury. (2023). *National Government Debt Recorded at P14.15 Trillion as of end-June 2023*. Retrieved from: https://www.treasury.gov.ph/wp-content/uploads/2023/08/NG-Debt-Press-Release-June-2023.pdf

Chee, L. (2023). Play and Counter-Conduct: Migrant Domestic Workers on TikTok. *Global Society: Journal of Interdisciplinary International Relations*, *37*(4), 593–617. https://doi.org/10.1080/13600826.2023.2217523

Cho, S., Crenshaw, K. W., & McCall, L. (2013). Toward a Field of Intersectionality Studies: Theory, Applications, and Praxis. *Signs*, *38*(4), 785–810. https://doi.org/10.1086/669608

Collins, P.H. (2000). *Black Feminist Thought: Knowledge, Consciousness, and the Politics of Empowerment*. Routledge. https://doi.org/10.4324/9780203900055

Collins, P.H. (2019). *Intersectionality as Critical Social Theory*. Durham, Duke University Press.

Coloma, R.S. (2008). Border crossing subjectivities and research: Through the prism of feminists of color. *Race, Ethnicity, and Education, 11*(1), 11–27.

Constantino, R., & Constantino, L. R. (1975). *A History of the Philippines: From the Spanish Colonization to the Second World War*. New York: Monthly Review Press.

de Guia, K. (2013). An ancient read of wholeness – The Babaylan. In L.M. Strobel's *Babaylan: Filipinos and the Call of the Indigenous*. Center for Babaylan Studies. https://www.amazon.ca/Babaylan-Indigenous-Leny-Mendoza-Strobel-ebook/dp/B09NM8ZTYY/ref=tmm_kin_swatch_0?_encoding=UTF8&qid=&sr=

de Leon, C. (2014). Family separation and reunification among former Filipina migrant domestic workers and their adult daughters in two Canadian cities in M. Romero, V. Preston, & W. Giles (Eds.), *When Care Work Goes Global: Locating the Social Relations of Domestic Work* (pp. 139–158). Ashgate.

Dhamoon, R. K. (2015). A feminist approach to decolonizing anti-racism: Rethinking transnationalism, intersectionality, and settler colonialism. *Feral Feminisms*, *4*, 20–37. https://feralfeminisms.com/wp-content/uploads/2015/12/ff_A-Feminist-Approach-to-Decolonizing-Anti-Racism_issue4.pdf

Enriquez, V. (1973). Kapwa: A concept in Filipino social psychology. In *From Colonial to Liberation Psychology*. Quezon City, Philippines: UP Press.

Enriquez, V. (1992). *From Colonial to Liberation Psychology*. Quezon City, Philippines: UP Press.

Francisco-Menchavez. (2018). *The Labor of Care: Filipina Migrants and Transnational Families in the Digital Age*. Urbana, Illinois, University of Illinois Press.

Friesen, J. (2011). The Philippines now Canada's top source of immigrants. *Globe and Mail.* Retrieved from: https://www.theglobeandmail.com/news/national/the-philippines-now-canadas-top-source-of-immigrants/article573133/

Jaggar, A.M. (2009). Transnational cycles of gendered vulnerability: A prologue to the Theory of global gender justice. *Philosophical Topics*, 33–52.

Kelly, P. (2014). *Understanding Intergenerational Social Mobility: Filipino Youth in Canada*. IRPP Study 45. Montreal: Institute for Research On Public Policy.

Kessler, C., & Rother, S. (2016). *Democratization through Migration?: Political Remittances and Participation of Philippine Return Migrants*. Lexington Books.

Lagmay, A. (1977). *Bahala na. Ulat ng Pambansang Samahan Sa Sikolohiyang Pilipino*, Quezon City, Philippines.

Le, A. N. (2022). Unanticipated transformations of infrapolitics. *The Journal of Peasant Studies*, *49*(5), 999–1018. https://doi.org/10.1080/03066150.2021.1888722

Lindio-McGovern, L. (2007). Neo-liberal Globalization in the Philippines: It's Impact on Filipino Women and Their Forms of Resistance. *Journal of Developing Studies*, *23*(1-2), 15–35.

Lutz, H. (2002). At Your Service Madam! The Globalization of Domestic Service. *Feminist Review*, *70*, 89–104. http://www.jstor.org/stable/1395972

Madison, D. S. (2005). *Critical Ethnography: Method, Ethics, and Performance*. Thousand Oaks, CA: SAGE.

Nagar, R., & Swarr, A. L. (2010). *Critical Transnational Feminist Praxis*. Albany: SUNY Press.https://library.smu.ca/login?url=https://search.ebscohost.com/login.aspx?direct=true&db=e000xna&AN=306680&site=ehost-live

Pande, A. (2012). From "Balcony Talk" and "Practical Prayers" to Illegal Collectives: Migrant Domestic Workers and Meso-Level Resistances in Lebanon. *Gender & Society*, *26*(3), 382–405. https://doi.org/10.1177/0891243212439247

Parreñas, R.S. (2004). The care crisis in the Philippines: Children and transnational families in the new economy. In B., Ehrenreich, & A.R, Hochschild (Eds.). *Global Woman: Nannies, Maids, and Sex Workers in the New Economy*(pp. 39–54). New York: Henry Holt and Company.

Pratt, G. (2012*). Families Apart: Migrant Mothers and Conflicts of Labour and Love*. Minneapolis, MN: University of Minnesota Press.

Roces, M. (2021). *The Filipino Migration Experience Global Agents of Change*. Cornell University Press. https://doi.org/10.1515/9781501760426

Sassen, S. (2004). Global cities and survival circuits. In B., Ehrenreich, & A.R, Hochschild (Eds.). *Global Woman: Nannies, Maids, and Sex Workers in the New Economy* (pp. 254–274). New York: Henry Holt and Company.

Sassen, S. (2008). Two stops in today's new global geographies shaping novel: Labor supplies and employment regimes. *American Behavioural Scientist*, *52*(3), 457–496.

Sassen, S. (2016). A massive loss of habitat: New drivers for migration. *Sociology of Development*, *2*(2), 204–233.

Ticar, J. E. (2017). Investigating the transnational identities of Filipina/o/x youth in Toronto urban high schools: A critical ethnographic study of the impact of Canada's live-in/caregiver program [Doctoral dissertation, University of Western Ontario]. Scholarship@Western. https://ir.lib.uwo.ca/etd/4951

Tuck, E. (2009). Suspending damage: A letter to communities. *Harvard Educational Review 79*(3), 409–428.

Tuck, E. & Yang, K. W. (2014). *Youth resistance research and theories of change*. Routledge, Taylor & Francis Group.

Tungohan, E. (2012). Debunking notions of migrant 'Victimhood': A critical assessment of temporary labour migration programs and Filipina migrant activism in Canada. In

R.S. Coloma., B. McElhinny, E. Tungohan, J.P.C. Catungal & L.M Davidson (Eds.), *Filipinos in Canada: Disturbing Invisibility*(pp.161–80), Toronto, ON: University of Toronto.

Tungohan, E. (2013). Reconceptualizing Motherhood, Reconceptualizing Resistance: Migrant Domestic Workers, Transnational Hyper-Maternalism and Activism. *International Feminist Journal of Politics*, *15*(1), 39–57. https://doi.org/10.1080/14616742.2012.699781

Tungohan, E. (2017). The transformative and radical feminism of grassroots migrant women's movement(s) in Canada. *Canadian Journal of Political Science/Revue Canadienne de Science Politique*, *50*(2), 479–494.

Tungohan, E. (2023). *Care activism : migrant domestic workers, movement-building, and communities of care*. University of Illinois Press.

Tungohan, E., Banerjee, R., Chu, W., Cleto, P., de Leon, C., Garcia, M., Kelly, P., Luciano, M., Palmaria, C., & Sorio, C. (2015). After the Live-In Caregiver Program: Filipina Caregivers' Experiences of Graduated and Uneven Citizenship. *Canadian Ethnic Studies*, *47*(1), 87–105. https://doi.org/10.1353/ces.2015.0008

Tyner, J.A. (1999). The global context of gendered labor migration from the Philippines to the United States. *American Behavioural Scientist*, *42(*4), 671–689.

4 Mobilizing the traumas of family separation and reunification through Vidaview Life Storyboards

Introduction

This chapter interrogates Filipina/o/x youths' narrations of 'trauma' through Tuck's (2009) 'desire-based research framework', which is "intent on depathologizing the experiences of dispossessed and disenfranchised communities so that people are seen as more than broken and conquered" (p. 416). Filipina/o/x youth navigate family separation and reunification through their political agency, making meaning of the "disorganized fragments" (p. 348) of their global migration experiences through the L/CP. They navigate these fragmented experiences of trauma through embodied activism (Johnson, 2023). Filipina mothers have mobilized the gendered vulnerabilities of Canada's Live-in/Caregiver Program (L/CP), impacting their children's global migratory trajectories. Like their mothers, Filipina/o/x youth continually make meaning of the traumas of family separation and reunification by coming to deeper understandings of their histories, memories, and emotions (Mohanty, 2003). Through political agency, Filipina mothers, their children, and school-community partnerships with Filipina/o/x community leaders co-resist against the structural violence of the L/CP (Bhuyan et al., 2018) which is transnationally embedded within the global domestic work industry.

I view political agency through the lens of embodied activism (Johnson, 2023), which can be defined as "the locus of intervention [that] stems precisely from the visceral immediacy of…interactions as the site of contested power" (p. 9). Filipina/o/x youth, like their mothers, mobilize the traumas of migration through their "embodied selves…in the navigation of social power relations and the creation of new possibilities" (Johnson, 2023, p. 9). Thus, Filipina/o/x youth and their mothers utilize their political agency, transforming their embodied experiences of family separation and reunification into advocacy sites, alongside school-community partnerships in Toronto urban schools. Employing critical arts-based inquiry (Finley, 2011) through verbal and non-verbal performances on the Vidaview Life Storyboard (Chase et al., 2012), a magnetic playboard used by researchers and clinicians, their lived experiences are centred and heard. A critical "arts-based inquiry is a strategic means for political resistance…it is a form of cultural resistance and a way to create a critical and dialogic space"

DOI: 10.4324/9781003287469-4

(Finley, 2011, p. 446). Thus, a critical arts-based inquiry through the Vidaview Life Storyboard showcases the political agency of Filipina/o/x youth, alongside their mothers and school community partnerships as co-resistors.

I conceive of school-community partnerships as transnational feminist spaces of co-resistance and praxis that mobilize the 'traumas' of family separation. Filipina/o/x community leaders, Filipina mothers, and Filipina/o/x youth engage in 'transnational feminist praxis' (Nagar & Swarr, 2010), which is understood as: "an intersectional set of…tools…and practices that…are shaped by a range of subjectivities and understandings of individual and collective agency" (p. 5). School-community partnerships facilitate processes of transnational feminist praxis with Filipina/o/x youth and Filipina mothers in social service provision, advocacy, and education where the programming "can feel profoundly affirming to be… [with] others whose bodies look and move like [their] own, especially if [they] often feel like the "deviant" body" (Johnson, 2023, p. 115) or the 'Other'.

Migration scholars investigating the impact of left behind children often highlight this "deviance" (Johnson, 2023), focusing on the traumatic impact of family separation within the global domestic work industry. It is important to note that family separation through global migration has led to significant psychological and emotional consequences among left-behind children (Bakker et al., 2009; Castañeda & Buck, 2011; de Leon, 2014; Pratt, 2010, 2012; Zentgraf & Chinchilla, 2012). Moreover, family separation has also led to other mental health concerns and low academic performance. Bakker et al. (2009) maintained that "many children left behind suffer from depression, low self-esteem, which can lead to behavioural problems, and [an] increased risk of poor academic performance as well as interruption of schooling" (p. 2). In the case of the L/CP, studies have demonstrated that Filipina/o/x youth in Canada have experienced low academic performance and high dropout rates from school as a result of family separation and the difficulties that arise from reunification (Farrales, 2017; Kelly, 2014; Pratt, 2010; 2012). Trauma as a result of family separation and reunification through the L/CP is violent (Pratt, 2012) and experiences should not be minimized. Nevertheless, this chapter also examines how Filipina/o/x youth mobilize these traumas as resistance so as "to refuse to be shaped on a body level by [oppression]" (Johnson, 2023, p. 114). These scholars provide context in understanding how the processes of family separation often lead to 'trauma' as well as how Filipina/o/x youth mobilize these lived experiences through embodied activism alongside their mothers and school-community partnerships.

Filipina/o/x youth

The Vidaview Life Storyboard (Chase et al., 2012) palpably captures "the affective and emotional geographies of transnationalism" (Dunn, 2010, p. 1) of the youth as they engaged in embodied activism within communities of care (Francisco-Menchavez, 2018) such as school-community partnerships. Francisco-Menchavez (2018) describes 'communities of care' as a "form of reorganizing care horizontally, *from* migrants *to* other migrants informed by their transnational familial context" (p. 97). School-community partnerships provide the transnational space for the youth and their mothers to engage in the emotional and affective depths of their lived experience through community care, where Filipina/o/x youth imagine how their future hopes and dreams would look like alongside their mothers and Filipina/o/x community leaders.

These relational aspects of transnational migration are important in understanding how Filipina/o/x youth mobilize the traumas of family separation through political agency. The Vidaview Life Storyboard (Chase et al., 2012) facilitates embodied activism (Johnson, 2023) as the youth unanimously shared that their mothers had left them behind to ensure that they had better economic and educational futures.

Table 4.1 represents the intersectional identities of the youth interviewed, where the majority had experienced family separation and reunification

Table 4.1 Intersectional identities of Filipina/o/x youth

Pseudonym	*Racial and gender self-identification (Filipina/o/x)*	*Age*	*Sexuality*	*Religion/ spirituality*	*Year of family separation*	*Year of family reunification*
Alicia	Filipina	18	Heterosexual	Christian	2007	2015
Angelica	Filipina	17	Heterosexual	Catholic	2008	2015
Anthony	Filipino	19	Heterosexual	Catholic	2005	2015
Bryan	Filipino	18	Questioning bi-sexuality	Catholic	2000	2013
Cara	Filipina	15	Heterosexual	Catholic	2008	2016
Chloe	Filipina	16	Heterosexual	Catholic	2008	2016
David	Filipino	16	Heterosexual	Catholic	2004	2016
Derek	Filipino	16	Heterosexual	Catholic	2014	2016
Edna	Filipina	17	Heterosexual	Catholic	2006	2015
Edgardo	Filipino	17	Heterosexual	Christian	2005	2015
Eric	Filipino	18	Homosexual	No religious identification	Unknown	2016
Ivy	Filipina	16	Heterosexual	Catholic	2008	2015
Jason	Filipino	16	Heterosexual	Catholic	n/a	n/a (arrived in 2013)
Joshua	Filipino	17	Heterosexual	Catholic	2006	2015
Juanito	Filipino	16	Heterosexual	Catholic	2005	2012
Marcelino	Filipino	16	Heterosexual	Catholic	2003	2016
Marsha	Filipina	17	Heterosexual	Catholic	Unknown	2016
Philip	Filipino	16	Heterosexual	Catholic	2001/2002 Unknown	n/a (arrived in 2016)
Rachel	Filipina	18	Heterosexual	Christian	n/a	n/a (arrived with family in 2015)
Rita	Filipina	17	Heterosexual	Catholic	2008	2015
Ricardo	Filipino	16	Heterosexual	Catholic	2006	2016
Rodrigo	Filipino	19	Heterosexual	Catholic	2007/2008 Unknown	2015

through the L/CP. There were a few youth such as Jason, Philip, and Rachel who did not experience family separation firsthand through the caregiver program, however, they were able to speak as witnesses and as newcomer youth to Canada. While Philip migrated with his mother to Canada in 2016, he did experience family separation when she worked in Hong Kong as a migrant domestic worker when he was an infant. Most of the youth identified as Roman Catholic & Christian, cisgendered, and heterosexual, while 2 youth identified as questioning bisexuality and homosexual and 1 youth as not having any religious affiliation.

Table 4.1 shows that the majority of youth have had long periods of separation, ranging from 2 to 13 years, before family reunification in Canada, providing context for the experiences of trauma. In the next section, I explore how the youth mobilize and navigate these experiences of trauma through embodied activism and political agency.

Mobilizing trauma and embodied activism

Researcher: You felt pain, emotionally?
Juanito: Cause she left me, right? I was kind of angry.
Researcher: Hurt?
Juanito: Yeah.

"She left me" are very powerful and palpable words that often resonated with the youth who had experienced family separation and reunification through the L/CP. Many of the youth exhibited 'fragments' (Pratt, 2010) in verbally expressing their global migration experiences, particularly around feeling "abandoned" when they were young children and were separated from their mothers. In October 2016, I had met with Juanito[1] (16 years old) after his classes were done for the day. He engaged with the Vidaview Life Storyboard (Chase et al., 2012) to explore his particular experience of family separation and reunification through the L/CP. Our meeting room then suddenly transformed into a sacred space that held Juanito's pain, anger, and hurt, where he inadvertently spoke back to the gendered vulnerabilities (Jaggar, 2009) and the structural violence (Bhuyan et al., 2018) his mother had experienced through Canada's L/CP. His emotions became the entry point to question, challenge, and mobilize the traumas of family separation and reunification. Moreover, his emotions were the catalysts to showcase his political agency through the subjectification (Foucault, 1980) of his experience, moving away from "deviance" (Johnson, 2023) and 'Otherness'. He engages in the "history, memory, emotion, and affectional ties [that] are significant elements of the construction of critical, self-reflective, feminist selves" (Mohanty, 2003, p. 8) within the contexts of transnational feminism in Toronto urban schools. Through the "Green Zone", the zone on "Families and Close Relations", on Vidaview Storyboard (VSB) (Chase et al., 2012), Juanito and the other youth mobilized their traumas through emotional and embodied transnationalism (Dunn, 2010).

Emotional and embodied transnationalism (Dunn, 2010) highlights how Filipina/o/x youth make meaning of the traumas of family separation and reunification through the verbal, written, and poetic performances of their political advocacy and agency. Moreover, the stories of Filipina/o/x youth "came…in a more disjointed form…distance from their mothers…the pain of leaving primary caregivers in the Philippines…these are difficult stories to tell (Pratt, 2010, p. 347). The Vidaview Life Storyboard (Vidaview Information Systems Ltd., 2012), verbal, written, and/or creative expression to engage in embodied activism (Johnson, 2023), navigating the traumas of prolonged family separation and demonstrating political agency on their own terms.

Upon reunification with his mother, Juanito had no other words to describe his feelings except that he felt "emotional". However, upon the utilization of the Vidaview Life Storyboard (Chase et al., 2012), he identified feelings of "pain", "hurt", and "anger" due to his feelings of abandonment when his mother left him behind in the Philippines. de Leon (2014) argued that "the moment of departure is an important moment to examine in the lives of children 'left behind' by migrant mothers, for the moments of departure signifies a moment of loss" (p. 147). This moment also signifies political agency and embodied activism as the youth mobilize the trajectory of losses encountered through the L/CP. Moreover, it looks at the ways in which co-resistance emerges. In terms of engaging within a community of care through school-community partnerships as a Filipina researcher, I was mindful of the difficulties of family separation and reunification, particularly the feelings of abandonment and the additional layers of loss when Filipina/o/x youth had left their extended families behind to migrate to Canada (Pratt, 2010), particularly their lolos and lolas (grandfathers and grandmothers), titas and titos (aunts and uncles) who had raised them while their mothers worked in the global domestic industry within transnational spaces.

Some of the youth did not know when or why their mothers had left them behind. Bryan, who was separated from his mother for 13 years, felt this loss as de Leon (2014) indicated above:

Bryan: She left while we were sleeping or she would think I was sleeping…So I opened my eyes and saw her crying.

Researcher: You saw her crying

Bryan: I didn't want to say anything because I thought I was in trouble so then she left, and I thought it was a dream so I slept again, but when I woke up, mom was gone, but it didn't really affect me too much because I thought she was just gonna come back... But, like after a year passed, I found out that she wasn't coming back, and I just kept it to myself. I never asked where she was. I never cried when she left because a part of me knew that she was doing it for us.

Bryan's experience represents both the individual and collective traumas of family separation and reunification due to family separation through the L/CP. These global migration traumas reinforce "one another, compounding the...sense of loss experienced" (Eyerman, 2019, p. 91). Despites these losses, the youth mobilize the trauma of family separation through their collective memories, which "refers to the selective and cumulative process through which collectivities...make use and meaningful sense of the past" (Eyerman, 2019, p. 147). These collectives include communities of care through school-community partnerships where Filipina/o/x youth, Filipina mothers, and Filipina/o/x community leaders engage in co-resistance and embodied activism.

Marsha, 17, appeared shy during our interview and answered questions with very short sentences and/or with a "yes" or "no." Although Marsha had very few words to say and our conversation lasted only 30 minutes, she powerfully expressed her embodied emotions within a transnational context (Dunn, 2010) when she narrated her experience of reunification with her mother at the airport:

Researcher: How was it like to see [your mom] again when...you came to Canada, how was it like when you saw her again? How did you feel?

Marsha: It's like my mom...I hug her...I miss her....I miss her.

Upon reflecting upon the moment of reunification, Marsha's love and affection for her mother was visible on her face when she repeated the words "I miss her". On her storyboard she drew two stick figures talking on the phone. One stick figure was situated in Canada and the other in the Philippines, and between these, she had used a magnet containing four hearts. Despite the distance during family separation, the love between mother–child remained steadfast. Marsha's drawing and affective statement "I miss her" demonstrated the "imagined and sensual-materiality" (Youkhana, 2015, p. 10) of transnational migration through the L/CP as she appeared to re-live the moment of hugging her mother during reunification. While the experience of family separation had been traumatic, Marsha also held valuable memories of family reunification. Her entangled and embodied experience of transnational, social, political, and cultural spaces were "re-articulated and re-negotiated" (Youkhana, 2015, p. 10) as she came to new understandings of what familial relations mean for her.

Filipina/o/x youth have experienced the 'traumas' family separation through the violence of the Canadian state where it's "arbitrary act[s] of sovereign power…defines [Filipina mothers] as less than citizen and temporarily strips them of their full personhood, including familial relations (Pratt, 2012, p. 70). Derek, aged 16, was one of the few youths to have reunified with his mother through the L/CP after two years. However, upon deeper exploration, this was not the first time experiencing family separation and reunification due to economic reasons as he had already experienced parental separation as a young child when his father left him behind to work in Korea:

Derek: When I was 7 years old, my father left the Philippines to earn money because our expenses were getting higher so we need more money to survive our daily lives.
Researcher: Do you know where he went?
Derek: I think it's Korea.

In 2011, Derek remembered experiencing family separation in multiple ways: 1) his parents separated and decided to end their marriage and 2) he experienced separation from his mother as she started to work in various global locations before migrating to Canada in 2014 through the L/CP:

Researcher: So, you talked about your dad…and how he left the Philippines because he needed to help with the finances. In 2014, your mom went to Canada. Do you understand why she had to go to Canada?
Derek: For the same reason, Miss. She's also gone to other places.
Researcher: Yeah, what places?
Derek: I don't really remember, Miss, cause I was still a kid at that time. I don't really remember.
Researcher: But you knew she went before…
Derek: Yes Miss, I know before she came to Canada, she went to Hong Kong. That's what I only remember.

I argue that Derek mobilizes his experience of 'trauma' in how he continually makes meaning of family relationships within multiple transnational contexts of family separation and reunification. For example, he saw his grandfather as a surrogate parent as a result of family separation and reunification enacted through the L/CP, where his grandfather performed as his caretaker when both his parents were physically absent.

Derek: My grandpa who already raised us is already dead, Miss.
Researcher: So that was tough too, hard?
Derek: Yes, because he was really supportive of us and everything… everything he supported us, he always supported us in everything, Miss. He prepare[d] our…lunch, he woke up early in the morning to cook our breakfast, it was like he was our mother and father.
Researcher: So he's like your parent?
Derek: Yeah.
Researcher: Ok, so, yeah, so there's lots of memories there, right, of your grandpa?
Derek: Five years or 6 [of memories of him looking after us]?

With transnational families, care is usually circulated among spouses and extended family members (Francisco-Menchavez, 2018). In Derek's situation, his grandfather became his main parental caregiver when both of his parents were not physically present. While many transnational children are usually excluded from decisions to migrate abroad for work (Hoang & Yeoh, 2015), Derek recalls either being informed somehow by someone or through his own observations of his parents' departures. Derek appeared to understand the reasons for his parents' global migration, which clearly impacted how he came to re-negotiate and understand the terms of his relationship with his grandfather who became his main caretaker for the last 5 or 6 years of his life. His relationship of transnational migration within his own family is complicated by the palpable grief that was clearly evident in his memory of his grandfather and what he meant to him as a significant and nurturing parental figure during those formative years when his parents were absent. What is significant here and how what struck me was the grief that emerged in Derek's response in relation to his sharing about the role and death of his grandfather in this affective element of the relational dynamic, which demonstrates his political agency when negotiating his experiences of trauma.

When Chloe's mother left the Philippines to work in Toronto, she and her family also experienced significant losses. Chloe's parents separated and she left her grandparents, her main caregivers, behind when she migrated to Canada. She navigates these losses and traumas through how she makes meaning of her relationship with her mother, one that oscillates between affection and her mom's distrust of her. An embodied memory she holds is the one of family reunification when she started crying and showing her mom affection when seeing her for the first time at the airport.

Ricardo, a 16 year old male who just had reunified with his mother in 2016, experienced similar affect upon family reunification, indicating, "When I saw my mom, I cried!" However, due to family separation for 10 years, the relationship with his mother is distant:

Ricardo: We talk but we're not going to do sweetness.
Researcher: Oh, it's like distant a little bit?
Ricardo: Distance, because when I do sweetness, [it's] awkward.

While the relationship with his mother is not close, this conversation speaks to the violence of the L/CP (Pratt, 2012) in that Ricardo and his mother were not able to establish and/or obtain a strong bond throughout the separation period. However, Ricardo navigates these entanglements when he first sees her at the airport and is filled with tears. His embodied emotions (Dunn, 2010) are indicative of the factors that need to shift within the L/CP: family separation.

For Rita, 17 years old, also experienced entangled and embodied emotions when she first reunified with her mother after 7 years, "I was shocked when she's already in front of me. I just wanted to hug her." Like many of newly reunified youth, Rita also experienced other forms of loss: "it's hard for me to accept that I'm going to stay…I didn't inform my friends, and even my father, he's still in the Philippines… it's kind of hard to adjust because I have no friends here" (Rita). Initially thinking that her migration to Canada would be temporary, she now realizes it is a permanent stay. She experiences joy and affection upon seeing her mother as well as the difficulties of being physically away from her friends and father in the Philippines.

Edna, 17 years old, still currently experiences an estranged relationship with her mother after 1 year of reunification in 2015. Moreover, she indicated on the Vidaview Life Storyboard that she is feeling "depressed" in relation to feeling "distant" from her mother. The affective dynamic of family separation speaks to a profound sense of abandonment, grief, and loss where "clinical depression and suicide are more serious examples of what can happen to youth who have experienced long-term separation from their migrant parents (de Leon, 2014, p. 152). While she indicated that the relationship with her mother still feels "distant", she also highlighted that her family is now "complete" as she and her mother are no longer physically separated. She also felt uncomfortable asking her mother to join the study because of how strained their relationship was at that time. Her storyboard depicted a gap between her and her mother, where she wrote "distant" and drew herself in close proximity to her father. She indicated that her father was her main caregiver while her mother was working in Canada. Edna engages in navigating the traumas of family separation and reunification, particularly her strained relationship with her mother. In attempting to secure economic futures through migration "parents and children who reunite after years of separation…find themselves to be strangers to each other" (Falicov, 2005, p. 401). Recently reunified youth also experience tense and distanced relationships due to the loss of intimacy and feelings of betrayal and frustration (de Leon, 2014). Nevertheless, a significant relationship for Edna is the one she has with her father, which remained steadfast during global migration (Figure 4.1).

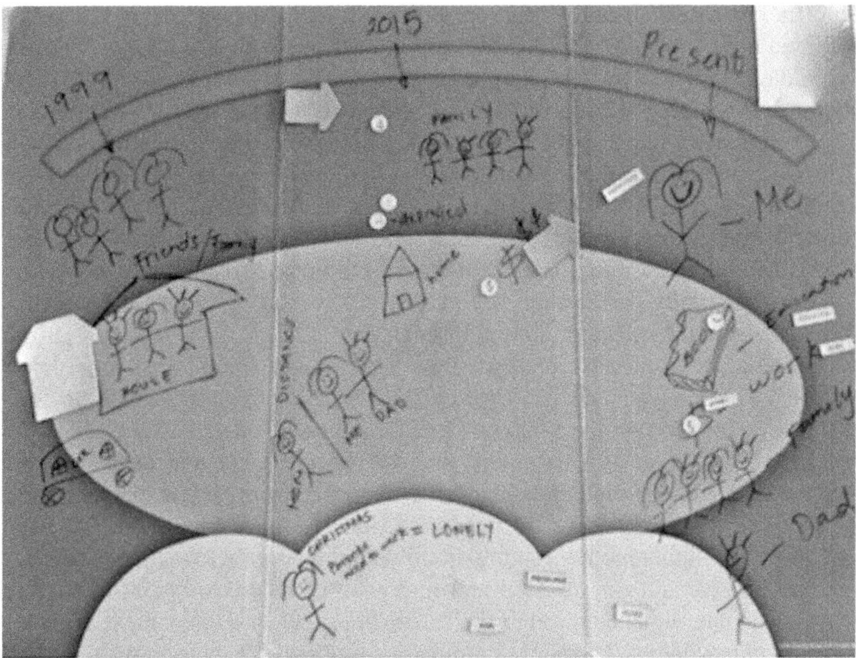

Figure 4.1 Edna's Vidaview Life Storyboard (Ticar, 2017)

In Cara's (15 years old) work on the Vidaview Life Storyboard, she revealed feelings of "shock", "loneliness", and that she missed her dad and friends who were left behind in the Philippines. A memory came up for her during our interview, "Mom had to go to Toronto for $$$$, for a brighter future, and for better education". Pratt (2012) describes these losses, in particular the traumas of family separation, where "mothers' and children's losses are irretrievable". Cara describes another form of trauma: Leaving her dad and friends behind while also trying to make sense of her mother leaving her behind for her educational and economic well-being. Similar to other youth, Cara left the Philippines without one of her caregivers, to reunite with their mothers who felt like "strangers" (Austria-Bonifacio, 2023; Falicov, 2005). Nevertheless, the youth, their mothers, and Filipina/o/x community leaders in school-community partnerships are co-resistors in that they facilitate future hopes and dreams of the youth through a 'desire-based' lens (Tuck, 2009), mobilizing the traumas of family separation through the L/CP collaboratively.

Future hopes and dreams as co-resistance

Filipina mothers, Filipina/o/x youth, and school-community partnerships are co-resistors in mobilizing the traumas of family separation through embodied activism. While the "separation of mothers from children is profoundly disruptive…

and…a chain of dislocations that are genuinely traumatic" (Pratt, 2012, p. 71), Filipina mothers have continually engaged in transnational mothering through technology during family separation, demonstrating care for their children that is far from neglect (Tungohan, 2013). They also provide for their families in the Philippines while also remaining engaged in civil society in their host countries (Tungohan, 2013). I argue that the transnational hopes and dreams Filipina mothers hold for their children are the ways in which they mobilize the traumas of family separation through political agency and embodied activism (Johnson, 2023). Additionally, Filipina/o/x youth and Filipina/o/x community leaders in school-community partnerships are part of this resistance against the violence on transnational families migrating through the L/CP.

Filipina/o/x youth have navigated the traumas and structural state violence of the L/CP (Bhuyan et al., 2018; Pratt, 2012), through "creative production" (Voicu, 2014, p. 9) on the Vidaview Life Storyboard. Cara, who was 15 at the time of reunification with her mother in 2016, reflected upon new insights on the relationship with her mother, which has transformed from feeling like they were "strangers" to a deep and heartfelt reconnection overtime. Trauma has impacted the lives of Filipina mothers and their children, however, transnational families are not passive and can develop new and positive relationships in the face of Canadian state violence through the L/CP (Pratt, 2012). This context provides deeper understanding(s) of how Filipina/o/x youth utilize their political agency to mobilize their 'traumas' where they "iteratively (re)turn…the subject as a moment of conclusion and control: a historically or contextually specific subject" (Bhabha, 1994, p. 186). Thus, Filipina/o/x, alongside their mothers and school-community partnerships, mobilize their traumas through embodied activism within the situated context of the L/CP.

Angelica was 17 years old when I first met her in 2016. At that time, she had recently reunified with her mother in 2015. Though she understood the economic reasons why her mother had left her and her brother, family separation had still left a deep emotional impact. She indicated that she always had a "good" relationship with her mother, she still struggled with some of the memories of family separation and being left-behind in the Philippines while her mother was in Canada. Exploring her memories, affect, and understanding of global migration, she voices her experience:

Angelica: I guess it's because most of us have been separated with our moms for a very long time and not everyone is, like, open-minded, not everyone understands the sacrifices that their parents made for them. That's what my mom is very proud of, like, me and my brother, like so open- minded, we have an understanding of what happened. Though, I don't know, sometimes I feel like something is missing.

Researcher: Yeah?

Angelica: Yeah cause you know like, she left us during our growing years so it's kinda of tough cause my brother is lucky I would say, I was the eldest, so I'm always there to support him and attend his meetings, like parent's meetings, I'm always the youngest one attending the meetings because I'm always there to support my brother because I don't want him to feel like he's not complete, like, I know how it feels so I don't want him to feel that way so I try my best to like give him everything that I don't have, and I don't know sometimes I realize that why my brother is so lucky that he feels everything that I want you know like, he has everything that I wished I had. You know, like the support, while growing up, no one supports me.

For Angelica, her experiences of "trauma" lie within the fact that her mother was not there for her in the way she needed while growing up, and consequently, she wanted to also shelter her brother from experiencing these feelings. While simultaneously understanding that her mother needed to leave for economic reasons, she became her brother's "protector", attending his parent-teacher meetings as her mother's proxy even though she is only a couple of years older. Some scholars, particularly in the field of Western psychology, would argue that Angelica became "parentified", when the child takes the role of the parent. Moreover, Bakker et al.'s (2009) argue that older siblings cope with the "difficulties of having to care for younger siblings" (pp. 9–10). However, Falicov (1998) argues that in collective cultures, like 'Latino' cultures, they stress "the duties of family members [who] help one another always" (p. 43), which applies to Angelica's situation where she is there for her brother when her mother cannot physically be there. This speaks to Angelica's political agency in the context of global and economic circumstances in the Philippines, as she helps out her mother and is there for her brother as a form of love, care, and protection.

Feeling like she did not have her emotional needs met while growing up speaks to the structural (Bhuyan et al., 2018) and state violence of the L/CP (Pratt, 2012) and how it is embedded with the gendered vulnerabilities (Jaggar, 2009) Filipina mothers. Angelica speaks back to this particular violence through her resistance to capitalist consumption and materialism:

> My mom would always send us money and let us buy anything that we want, new clothes, new shoes, gadgets, foods, like any foods that we want…I realized that it's really not about the material thing(s), it's really like what matters the most is your family being together.
>
> (Angelica)

Angelica speaks about her need for family connection, which she values over material goods. This is resistance is important in addressing the impact of the

L/CP on Filipina/o/x youth. Moreover, the violence of gendered vulnerabilities (Jaggar, 2009) continually impacts Filipina/o/x youth after reunification. As a result of Natalia joining the global workforce, Angelica became her brother's caregiver in the Philippines and in Canada. Nevertheless, Angelica is keenly aware of Natalia's struggles as a working-class single mother who now works long hours at a factory to make ends meet. Angelica explained that "here in Toronto, money's a problem cause my dad died when we were kids". This insight is key to Angelica's embodied activism and political agency, particularly when mobilizing the traumas of the L/CP.

In a follow-up study with Angelica's family, including Natalia and Brandon, her younger brother in 2022, Angelica mobilizes her traumas of 7 years family separation shared through all of their attempts to reconnect with one another on a deeper and affective level. Falicov (2005) argues that emotional aspects associated with the experiences of transnational migration are an important consideration in moving to an understanding about the impact of such forms of globalization. Under these conditions of separation, contact via social media, rather than physically through daily interaction, can create an extended heart across geographical space: "because lives and relations are linked across borders, transnationalism offers an attractive, and at times deceiving, imagined possibility of living with two hearts rather than with one divided heart" (p. 339). However, Pratt (2012) had a different take on children who have been separated from their mothers due to the L/CP as "transnational mothering cannot transcend distance…[and] communication is often infrequent, and inevitably fragmented and stripped of the sensuality of day-to-day, face-to-face, embodied contact" (p. 70). Angelica's experience resonates with both Falicov's (2005) Pratt's (2012) perspectives because while Angelica started with deeper understanding(s) of gender and global migration processes through the L/CP and maintained a fairly good relationship with her mother during family separation and after reunification, it took collective effort to emotionally reconnect with her mother in an embodied way.

Anthony, a 19-year-old Filipino, shared: "I was pretty happy to see my mom because it's not really a good thing that you haven't seen your mother, parent, for a long time, but we did Skype [during family separation]." In his Vidaview Life Storyboard, he depicted his mother as "superwoman" who is providing continual financial support to 4 children here in Canada while his father is in the Philippines:

Researcher: How was it like to see your mom again in 2015?

Anthony: When I was smaller, I expected my mom to be taller and bigger because parents usually are bigger than their children but nothing has changed with mom but she was shorter.

Researcher: Or maybe you grew?

Anthony's storytelling appeared to be "fragmented" (Pratt, 2010), and I did not press for exact details of events as I was mainly concerned about how he navigated the complex pieces of family separation and reunification. He points out his mothers political agency through his perception of her migration experience, a "superwoman" despite the 'gendered vulnerabilities' (Jaggar, 2009) within a state violent embedded immigration program such as the L/CP (Pratt, 2012). Anthony's imaginative connection of his mother's migration experience to her superhuman qualities speaks to how Anthony "explores…a line of inquiry… to understand the specific historical circumstances and regimes of power under which [he] is made diasporic in the first place (Mohapatra, 2006, p. 3).

While he was partially joking that his mother "shrank," it speaks to the 10 years of family separation and how she has become unrecognizable upon reunification. Interestingly, Anthony represented her as a "superwoman," signifying her strength rather than her gendered vulnerabilities (Jaggar, 2009), providing a nuanced perspective around how, "few separated youths could perform a heroic narrative and [how] their stories came less easily and in a more disjointed form" (Pratt, 2010, p. 347). Anthony's narrative depicts how transnational Filipina/o/x families are not victims of difficult global circumstances (Pratt, 2012).

David, a 16-year-old Filipino boy who reunified with his mother in 2016 after 12 years of family separation. On his Vidaview Life Storyboard, he engaged in embodied activism through affect and poetics, "words are placed on a page in poetic form to include the performative dimension of a speaker" (Madison, 2012, p. 239). As David recalled leaving his loved ones behind in the Philippines and subsequently crying as result, he performed through the senses in the most palpable manner the feelings of loss, grief, and abandonment. It was clear that the separation had impacted him deeply and he was ok to continue on with the conversation despite the tears. He indicated that his tears were part of the expression of his sadness as a consequence of being separated from his mother:

> We kept contact by using social media, and as time goes by, it's like I'm drifting away from my mom and [getting] closer to my grandparents. When I saw my mom go back (voice trembling) it was like she was just not there. I didn't really feel anything, I only felt one thing, because I wouldn't be able to see my grandparents anymore (crying). Everyone back home thinks it's easy to be away from your loved ones, and now I know how my mom felt when she left us.
>
> (David, personal interview)

David's poetic expression of his migration experience was by no means "thin" or "fragmentary" (Pratt, 2010), and his narrative speaks to the difficulty of leaving his caregivers in the Philippines upon reunification with his mother in Canada. His use of poetics and embodied activism, "joins …the mutual importance of *how* something is said along with *what* is said…The narrative event and narrated event coalesce in a poetic rendering" (Madison, 2012, p. 34). In David's narrative performance, he shows how he feels through writing and through tears as he "presents to us one moment *of* history, and how that moment *in* history is *remembered* through a *particular* subjectivity" (emphasis in original) (Madison, 2012, p. 35).

Ivy, a 16 year old Filipina who reunified with her mother in 2015, did not express pain when leaving her caregivers in the Philippines behind when she immigrated to Canada as they were the ones who misused the remittances that were to be used for her daily needs:

Researcher: When you were in the Philippines and your mom left to Saudia Arabia, were the rest of your family in the Philippines?

Ivy: At first, it was just the three of us, without my dad because my dad was also in Saudi and later on when my parents found out that, like when our guardian, [who is] our cousin and…found out they were stealing the money that our parents were trying to give us that's when my dad decided to go back to the Philippines and then take care of us.

Researcher: So you weren't given the money that was supposed to be given to you and how did you find out? Like, what happened?

Ivy: Cause when my mom was trying to update the expenses, whenever she sends us money to the Philippines and asks for expenses, it's like it's been just a week and then my cousin is like saying that oh we don't have any more money, something like that.

Ivy's parents entrusted Ivy's cousin to become her guardian and to take care of the household finances and childcare. However, the very act of her cousin misusing the money speaks to experiences of family betrayal where, "migration shakes up the family social structure…since those left behind make up for the unpaid house work and decision-making…missing parent(s) would have done otherwise" (Castañeda & Buck, 2011, p. 102). Though migration has changed Ivy's family social structure resulting in her cousin becoming the entrusted guardian, Ivy's dad became present as soon as the trust was broken and remittances became "a financial household strategy having implications that expand far beyond the realm of the economic to affect social roles and emotional processes such as…gender formation" (Castañeda & Buck, 2011, p. 102). Ivy's father then became the caregiver and consequently, Ivy mobilized her experiences with family betrayal and remittances into feeling "blessed" when she reunified with her mother in Canada and her father in the Philippines.

Researcher: How was it like to see your mom again?

Ivy: I feel blessed.

Researcher: *Because you didn't see her for a while, right?*

Ivy: *Mh hmm.*

Researcher: *How about the successes of your family?*

Ivy: *You see how each part of the family does their work so that's what makes it successful for example, we got a car, and we help each other in terms of expenses and stuff like that...for health, let's say mental health, like when you feel down, they'll be there to listen to you, stuff like that.*

Researcher: So lots of support, so how about some failures?

Ivy: When you fail, they're still there to support you and [if] you do any mistakes, they're by your side to guide you.

Researcher: And you have the money symbol?

Ivy: For me, I have a job now, so I don't rely on my parent's anymore, so things that could help, instead of giving the money to me, they could just spend it more on our food.

Through political agency, Ivy mobilizes the losses of family separation and betrayal by highlighting the successes of family reunification, specifically the reciprocity evident among her familial relations. Ivy's experience showcases that mobilizing traumas produce opportunities and possibilities during the reunification period through embodied activism and political agency.

School-community partnerships, Filipina/o/x youth, and Filipina mothers: communities of care

Filipina/o/x community leaders within school-community partnerships facilitate communities of care among Filipina mothers and Filipina/o/x youth as co-resisters against the structural violence (Bhuyan et al., 2018) and Canadian state violence of the L/CP (Pratt, 2012). School-community partnerships facilitate the mobilization of the gendered vulnerabilties of the global domestic work industry (Jaggar, 2009) in Canada and the traumas of family separation through the L/CP. I argue that school-community partnerships engage in transnational feminism and praxis as a means to facilitate the political agency of Filipina mothers and Filipina/o/x youth, particularly in how they co-resist against the "practices of globalization and capitalist patriarchies" (Nagar & Swarr, 2010, p. 5) of the L/CP and its impacts on transnational families as demonstrated by the Filipina/o/x youth in the previous section. Through the embodied activism (Johnson, 2023) of 'communities of care' (Francisco-Menchavez, 2018), Filipina/o/x community leaders with school-community partnerships facilitate the political agency of Filipina/o/x youth by assisting them to "grapple with the complex and contradictory ways in which these processes both inform and are shaped by… understandings of individual and collective agency" (Nagar & Swarr, 2010, p. 5).

School-community partnerships engage in transnational political practice contingent upon building solidarity across divisions, which globalization makes it difficult but also offers up possibilities (Mohanty, 2003). de Leon (2014) argued that community activism, "enabled [Filipina/o/x youth] to build lasting bonds of friendship with other Filipino migrant families but most importantly, nurtured possibilities of post-reunification reconciliation between themselves and their mothers" (p. 9). School-community partnerships facilitate these processes of transnational feminist praxis where they provide supportive space(s) to understand the underlying political reasons for their mothers leaving them in the first place, "involvement in…community projects aimed at fighting against discriminatory Canadian foreign policies helped [to] name…childhood pain and understand the structural causes behind it" (de Leon, 2014, p. 151). Therefore, school-community partnerships play a significant role in mobilizing the traumas of family separation through the political agency and embodied activism of Filpina mothers and Filipina/o/x youth.

Gaining knowledge around the empowering role of school-community partnerships such as the Newcomer Support Centre (NSC) and the Services for a Diverse Community (SDC) in educational systems is important as they facilitate the agency of Filipina/o/x youth as "these contingencies are often the grounds of historical necessity for elaborating empowering strategies of emancipation…it requires…rearticulation…in which cultural identities may be inscribed (Bhabha, 1994, p. 171). School-community partnerships provide space for Filipina/o/x youth to negotiate their experiences of the traumas through "the…intervention of something that takes on new meaning…[and] emerges [in] the process of agency both as a historical development as the narrative agency of historical discourse (Bhabha, 1994, p. 191). Thus, through their embodied experience and the interventions of communities of care, Filipina/o/x youth engage in the process of political agency and the negotiation of their experiences of trauma.

Conclusion

This chapter highlighted how school-community partnerships facilitate the mobilization of traumas among Filipina/o/x youth through the praxis of communities of care (Francisco-Menchavez, 2018), including a sense of 'place-belongingness', or a feeling of being 'at home' (Antonsich, 2010). School-community partnerships are the socio-spatial location in which to engage in the processes of making sense of 'diaspora', connecting "collectivities and communities which extend across geographical spaces and historical experiences. There are a vast number of people who exist in one place and yet feel intimately related to another" (Cho, 2007, p. 13). This was evident throughout the chapter as the youth spoke about their memories of family separation and reunification as a diasporic community, co-resisting the gendered vulnerabilities and traumas of the L/CP alongside their mothers and school-community partnerships with Filipina/o/x leaders.

The chapter also provided some insight into how Filipina/ox youth engage in political agency through their cultural memories and emotions, specifically the traumas of family separation and reunification. Embodying a subjectification processes (Hall, 1996), Filipina/o/x youth utilize their political agency through the making-meaning of culturally-specific symbols such as, "literature, art, music ritual, life, death…[the production] of meanings…[that] circulate as signs within specific contextual locations and social systems of values" (p. 172). Moreover, they mobilize the traumas of family separation and reunification experienced through the L/CP through the Vidaview Life Storyboard through signs and symbols representing their memories, political agency, and embodied activism.

While this chapter focused on mobilizing the traumas of family separation and reunification among Filipina/o/x youth in Toronto urban schools, particularly their memories family separation through the L/CP, the next chapter focuses on exploring "diaspora", their intersectional identities, and making meaning of their transnational homes. Furthermore, it looks how political agency, embodied activism, and co-resistance among Filipina/o/x leaders, Filipina/o/x youth, and Filipina mothers through school-community partnerships play a contingent role in facilitating how Filipina/o/x youth make meaning and negotiate their diasporic identities as transnational youth.

Note

1 The names of all of the Filipina/o/x youth have been changed to pseudonyms throughout this chapter.

References

Antonsich, M. (2010). Searching for belonging: An analytical framework. *Geography Compass*, *4*(6), 644–659.

Austria-Bonifacio, J. (2023). *Reuniting with strangers : A novel*. Douglas & McIntyre.

Bakker, C., Elings-Pels, M., & Reis, M. (2009). *The impact of migration on children in the Caribbean*. UNICEF.

Ball, J. (2020). An arts-based, peer-mediated Story Board Narrative Method in research on identity, belonging and future aspirations of forced migrant youth. *Migration, Mobility & Displacement*, 5(1), 83–93. https://doi.org/10.18357/mmd51202019628

Bhabha, H. K. (1994). *The location of culture*. Routledge.

Bhuyan, R., Valmadrid, L., Panlaqui, E. L., Pendon, N. L., & Juan, P. (2018). Responding to the structural violence of migrant domestic work: Insights from participatory action research with migrant caregivers in Canada. *Journal of Family Violence*, *33*(8), 613–627. https://doi.org/10.1007/s10896-018-9988-x

Castañeda, & Buck (2011). Remittances, transnational parenting, and the children left behind: Economic and psychological implications. *The Latin Americanist*, *55*, 85–110.

Cho, L. (2007). The turn to diaspora. *TOPIA*,17.

de Leon, C. (2014). Family separation and reunification among former Filipina migrant domestic workers and their adult daughters in two Canadian. In cities in M. Romero, V. Preston, & W. Giles (Eds.), *When care work Goes global: Locating the social relations of domestic work* (pp. 139–158). Ashgate.

Dunn, K. (2010). Embodied transnationalism: Bodies in transnational spaces. *Population, Space and Place*, *16*, 1–9.

Eyerman, R. (2019). *Memory, trauma, and identity*. Palgrave Macmillan.

Falicov, C. J. (1998). *Latino families in therapy: A guide to multicultural practice*. Guilford Press.

Falicov, C. J. (2005). Emotional transnationalism and family identities. *Family Process*, *44*(4), 399–406. https://doi.org/10.1111/j.1545-5300.2005.00068.x

Farrales, M. (2017). Delayed, deferred and dropped out: Geographies of Filipino-Canadian high school students. *Children's Geographies*, *15*(2), 207–223. https://doi.org/10.1080/14733285.2016.1219020

Finley, S. (2011). Critical arts-based inquiry: The pedagogy and performance of a radical ethical aesthetic. In N. Denzin, & Y. Lincoln (Eds.), *The SAGE handbook of qualitative research*. 4th ed. (pp. 435–450). SAGE.

Foucault, M. (1980). *Power/knowledge: Selected interviews and other writings 1972-1977*. C. Gordon (Ed). Pantheon Books.

Francisco-Menchavez (2018). *The labor of care: Filipina migrants and transnational families in the digital age*. University of Illinois Press.

Hall, S. (1996). *Questions of cultural identity*. SAGE.

Hoang, L. A., & Yeoh, B. S. A. (2015). Children's agency and its contradictions in the context of transnational labour migration from Vietnam. Global Networks, 15(2), 180–197. doi: 10.1111/glob.12057

Hirschberger, G. (2018). *Collective trauma and the social construction of meaning. Frontiers in Psychology*, *9*, 1441–1441.https://doi.org/10.3389/fpsyg.2018.01441

Jaggar, A. M. (2009). Transnational cycles of gendered vulnerability: A prologue to the theory of global gender justice. *Philosophical Topics*, 33–52.

Johnson, R. (2023). *Embodied activism engaging the body to cultivate liberation, justice, and authentic connection: A practical guide for transformative social change*. North Atlantic Books.

Kelly, P. (2014). *Understanding intergenerational social mobility: Filipino Youth in Canada*. IRPP Study 45. Institute for research on public policy.

Madison, D. S. (2012). *Critical ethnography: Method, ethics, and performance* (2nd ed.). SAGE.

Mohanty, C. T. (2003). *Feminism without borders: Decolonizing theory, practicing solidarity*. Duke University Press.

Mohapatra, A. K. (2006). The paradox of return: Origins, home and identity in M.G. Vassanji's *The Gunny Sack. Postcolonial Text*, *2*(4), 1–21.

Nagar, R., & Swarr, A. L. (2010). *Critical transnational feminist praxis*. SUNY Press.

Pratt, G. (2010). Listening for spaces of ordinariness: Filipino-Canadian youths' transnational lives. *Children's Geographies*, *8*(4), 343–352.

Pratt, G. (2012*). Families apart: Migrant mothers and conflicts of labour and love*. University of Minnesota Press.

Ticar, J. E. (2017). *Investigating the Transnational Identities of Filipina/o/x Youth in Toronto Urban High Schools: A Critical Ethnographic Study of the Impact of Canada's Live-In/Caregiver Program*. ProQuest Dissertations & Theses.Tuck, E. (2009). Suspending damage: A letter to communities. *Harvard Educational Review*, 79(3), 409–428.

Tuck, E. (2009). Suspending damage: A letter to communities. *Harvard Educational Review*, *79*(3), 409–428.

Tungohan, E. (2013). Reconceptualizing Motherhood, Reconceptualizing Resistance Migrant domestic workers, transnational hyper-maternalism and activism. *International Feminist Journal of Politics*, 15(1), 39–57. https://doi.org/10.1080/14616742.2012.699781

Voicu, C.-G. (2014). *Exploring cultural identities in jean Rhys' fiction*. De Gruyter.

Youkhana, E. (2014). Creative activism and art against urban renaissance and social exclusion - space sensitive approaches to the study of collective action and belonging. *Sociology Compass*, *8*(2), 172–186. https://doi.org/10.1111/soc4.12122

Youkhana, E. (2015). A conceptual shift in studies of belonging and the politics of belonging. *Social Inclusion*, *3*(4), 10–24.

Zentgraf, K. M., & Chinchilla, N. S. (2012). Transnational family separation: A framework for analysis. *Journal of Ethnic and Migration Studies*, *38*(2), 345–366. doi: 10.1080/1369183X.2011.646431.

5 Negotiating intersectional identities through group art projects

Introduction

> I used to believe that, like, my skin colour is not beautiful because it's in mainstream that people who have fair skin are much [more] beautiful.
>
> (Rita)[1]

Rita, a 17-year-old transnational Filipina student in grade 12 had reunited with her mother in 2015 through the L/CP. She initially seemed reserved in speaking about her experiences, though she appeared to be more comfortable as the interview unfolded. When I asked her, "How about skin colour, does that matter to some people?" Rita then spoke about how she has experienced racism and acknowledges that, "Yeah, [skin colour] really matters cause they call me 'black' in the Philippines….there is…racism." The colourism and racism to which Rita refers above is rooted in colonialism: "Spain introduced colorism… colorism and then racism inculcated the notions such as: 'White is beautiful,' 'White is intelligent,' and 'White is powerful' in the psyches of many brown-hued Filipinos, thus inferiorizing the Filipino" (Pierce, 2005, p. 33).

In navigating the impact of colonialism and systemic racism, Rita, like the other Filipina/o/x youth, has exhibited political agency as she comes to an understanding between skin colour discrimination, colonialism, and systemic racism. Rita's "process of subjectification is an ongoing and situated negotiation of self-naming and being named by others that relies on visible and non-visible markers of difference and is implicated in power relations" (Coloma, 2008, p. 20). As Coloma argued, this process of subjectification has emerged from a constituted framework that "has to contend with the available socio-historical discourses that regulate positions and meanings" (p. 21). This chapter looks at the impact of colonization on the intersectional identities of Filipina/o/x youth and how they in turn, engage in decolonization, political agency, and subjectification processes through their understandings of how race, class, gender, sexuality, religion, and spirituality have impacted their identities. Furthermore, it focuses on the politics of belonging and the role Filipina/o/x youth play as agentic subjects in making-meaning of their transnational experiences, family relations, and the level of their school engagement.

DOI: 10.4324/9781003287469-5

This chapter is mainly concerned with how intersectional, "identities interplay, mutually shape each other, and affect experiences of privilege and oppression" (Coloma, 2008, p. 21). I employ such a framework to address how race, class, gender, sexuality, religion and spirituality, "intersect and interact with each other, across contexts, [and] affect social identity and lived experiences" (Goodman & Jackson, 2012, p. 234). Mapping these particular social ontologies, "to where sets of relations are situated, manifested in categories and materialized in concrete relations" (Anthias, 2011, p. 6), I situate Filipina/o/x youth's agency in relation to the colonial history of the Philippines, their school experiences, their mothers' migration experiences, and their intersectional identities.

Making-meaning of transnational 'home'

Derek, 16, utilizes his political agency to make meaning of 'home' as a transnational Filipino student in a Toronto urban school. In this context, home, "is not a place that one leaves behind, but a geographical point of reference, a sense of place that serves as an anchor" (Voicu, 2014, p. 25). Entangled in his global migration experience through the L/CP, he navigates his sense of identity and belonging in the Philippines and in Canada:

> When I first came, I was like, this is Canada! But when time passes, it's like you miss your home, you want to go back to your home because you miss your cousins, the places, the environment here and there is different cause I grew up there and I am only new here. So it's still my home, even though I'm here, it's like that. So maybe this is already my home because I'm already here but I still consider [the] Philippines as my home.
>
> (Derek)

For Derek, the Philippines is his transnational home and a point of reference that has shaped his cultural understandings of his intersectional identity. He feels an emotional and affective sense of belonging (Antonsich, 2010) to this situated geographical location due to familial and community relations. However, he also indicates that Canada is his now his 'home' because he is physically present, implying that he is navigating the politics of belonging (Yuval-Davis, 2011) as a racialized newcomer through his political agency. Derek's global migration experience highlights the following questions: "what becomes the sense of home? Is home merely a place to depart from, or can we see travel as leading us to think about how homes must be cultivated through movement?" (Voicu, 2014, p. 25), demonstrating that his sense of belonging as a diasporic Filipino constantly transforms as he navigates different situated contexts (Mohapatra, 2006) such in Canada and the Philippines.

While utilizing his political agency to navigate his transnational identity and belonging in Toronto urban schools, he is "caught between the homes 'there' and 'here'...What emerges from the context of the ambiguity of home...is a set of broader issues:...how momentous histories of nation-states are deconstructed through private experiences, memories, and strategies...they all seem to revolve around the diasporic subject's engagement with issues of origin and identity" (Mohapatra, 2006, p. 3). Derek navigates his transnational identity and belonging, which are contingent upon the impact of family separation and reunification through the L/CP.

In Derek's depiction of home through visual representation, he imagined being far away from geographically from his loved ones yet physically located within the Canadian nation-state. Moreover, he had left his loved ones behind in the Philippines but remains connected through the notion of 'diaspora', which is "first and foremost a subjective condition marked by the contingencies of long histories of displacements and genealogies of dispossession...they emerge in...turning back upon those markers of self – homeland, memory, loss" (Cho, 2007, p. 11). Derek engages in this political agency through the navigation of his transnational home as well as family separation in multiple ways. On one hand, he has been displaced from family and has faced multiple losses, such as the memories of his grandfather and the grief that emerged from his death during his migration experience. On the other hand, he is in the process of making meaning of his identity and belonging in Toronto urban schools, demonstrating his political agency about his "subjective accounts of [his] thoughts, feelings, and acts about [his mothers' migration" (Hoang & Yeoh, 2015, p. 193).

Intersectional identities

Derek engages in political agency through his memory and losses of global migration. Throughout this process, Derek engages in the complex power relations entangled with the "social, imagined, and sensual-material relations that are constantly re-articulated and re-negotiated by actors in their day-to-day practices" (Youkhana, 2015, p. 10). He engages in 'place-belonging', the "personal, intimate feeling of belonging to a place [and] come[s] to terms with discourses and practices of socio- spatial inclusion/exclusion at play in that very place" (Antonsich, 2010, p. 649). Filipina/o/x youth make meaning of their place-belonging that are contingent upon the power relations embedded in this culture, which is utilized as socio-historical space(s) for Filipina/o/x youth to make sense of their identity and belonging in Toronto urban schools:

> Culture as a strategy of survival is both transnational and translational. It is transnational because contemporary postcolonial discourses are rooted in specific histories of cultural displacement...culture is translational because such spatial histories of displacement...make the question of how culture signifies, or what is signified by *culture,* a rather complex issue.
>
> (Bhabha, 1994, p. 172)

In the latter part of the chapter, I discuss the individual and collective cultural representation of how they make meaning of their intersectional identities through group art projects. These group art projects represent how they make sense of home-making through political agency and the "creative production of *diasporic hybridity* take[ing] the form of a delicate double-matter: denial and appropriation as such in the name of perennial 'homelessness' and at the same time engaging in the polemical politics of representation" (Voicu, 2014, p. 9). These aspects of 'diasporic hybridity' are explored through intersectionality, which can be described as: "a critique of gender and race-based research for failing to account for the lived experience at neglected points of intersection – ones that tended to reflect multiple subordinate locations as opposed to dominant or mixed locations" (McCall, 2005, p. 1780). Mutual constitutive intersectionality entails that each particular social category, such as race, class, gender, sexuality, religion, and spirituality, cannot have the same political meaning(s) as another category and cannot be reduced to having the same meaning; the political role of intersectional analysis is to make visible seemingly invisible inequalities and inequities, but this does not mean these categories solely define people (Yuval-Davis, 2012). Moreover, there are three important points of analyses within this chapter:

> First, while people can identify exclusively with one identity category… their concrete social location is constructed along multiple axes of difference…Second, the intersecting social divisions cannot be analysed as items that are added up but, rather, as constituting each other. Third, the question of describing social location in terms of certain specific grids of difference is far from simple…there are some social divisions that are more important than others in constructing individuals' specific positionings… the construction of categories of signification is, in the last instance, a product of human creative freedom and autonomy. Without specific social agents who construct and point to certain analytical and political features, the other members of society would not be able to identify them.
>
> (Yuval-Davis, 2006, pp. 200–201)

Filipina/o/x youth have identified the multiple axes of difference that are mutually-constituted (Yuval-Davis, 2006), that have impacted their intersectional identities. Through a visual art performance, the group art project irreducibly looks at the youths' social locations as well as their "identifications and emotional attachments to various collectivities and groupings [and their]… ethical and political value systems with which people judge their own and others' belonging/s" (Yuval-Davis, 2006, p. 199).

'Markers of difference'

Hall (1996) argues that racial identities have been constructed through a discourse of inferiorization and white superiority, in "specific historical and institutional sites...within the play of specific modalities of power, and thus are more the product of the marking of difference and exclusion" (p. 4). Colourism and systemic racism involve "not only [the]construction of boundaries but also the inclusion or exclusion of particular people, social categories and groupings within these boundaries by those who have the power to do this" (Yuval-Davis, 2011, p. 18). According to Yuval-Davis (2011), the politics of belonging includes "not only the maintenance and reproduction of boundaries of the community of belonging by the hegemonic political powers (within and outside the community), but also their contestation, challenge, and resistance by other political agents (Yuval-Davis, 2011, p. 20). This chapter examines the ways in which Filipina/o/x youth engage in 'resistance' and political agency in relation to their intersectional identities and their "pivotal [relationship] to a politics of location...By 'agency'...it seems to be in the attempt to rearticulate the relationship between subjects and discursive practices that the question of identity recurs (Hall, 1996, p. 2). I maintain, then, that Filipina/o/x engage in 'resistance' to systemic racism by utilizing their political agency to negotiate their intersectional and transnational identities in Toronto urban schools.

In the previous chapter, I highlighted how Filipina/o/x youth have mobilized the traumas of family separation and reunification through political agency and embodied activism, while this chapter illuminates their understanding(s) of family separation and reunification in relation to their intersectional identities and how they make meaning of 'home'. Moreover, Filipina/o/x youth demonstrate their political agency and co-resistance with their mothers by envisioning hopes and dreams through future successes, which they all identified in the group art project. Notwithstanding the need for equitable interventions within educational and immigration policies and practices to address systemic oppression through school-community partnerships, Filipina/o/x youth and their mothers navigate the meaning of transnational 'homes' in relation to their intersectional identities and sense of belonging in Toronto urban schools.

Agency: Identity and belonging

Political agency

The situated and transnational context(s) provide deeper understanding(s) of how Filipina/o/x youth navigate their intersectional identities and takes "into account...how...the ability of those 'left-behind' to exercise agency is closely intertwined with processes of social becoming and navigation in the transnational social fields constructed for them by adults" (Hoang & Yeoh, 2015, p. 180). In Chapter 3, Filipina mothers describe how they mobilize the gendered vulnerabilities (Jaggar, 2009) and the structural and state violence of the L/CP (Bhuyan et al., 2018; Pratt, 2012). The political agency of Filipina mothers has impacted the ways in which Filipina/o/x youth make meaning of their intersectional identity and belonging in Toronto urban schools.

While left-behind transnational youth may exhibit aspects of 'powerlessness', they also demonstrate 'power', "it would be a mistake to infer that children left behind are consequently powerless…To the contrary…their…reactions…ultimately shape families' migration trajectories when parents make subsequent migratory decisions grounded in their children's responses" (Dreby, 2007, p. 1062). This chapter looks at the ways in which migration has impacted Filipina/o/x youth and the 'power' they hold as they navigate their transnational identities through their political agency. Moreover, it looks at the "complex entanglements of young people's lives with…nuanced analyses of the specific, contextual relations and identities that inform their sense of citizenship" (Hörschelmann & El Refaie, 2014, p. 444) as transnational youth in Toronto urban schools whose "political understandings and perspectives [have been influenced by their] relationships with family and friends across distances" (Hörschelmann & El Refaie, 2014, p. 445).

The group art project provided collective understandings of Filipina/o/x youths' intersectional identities "as a means of strengthening their cultural identity and sense of belonging" (Lee, 2016, p. 2573), in collaboration with school-community partnerships with Filipina/o/x leaders and Filipina mothers. The group art project highlighted a collective sense of transnational identity and belonging as, "paying attention to young people's own accounts of their agency helps illuminate important aspects of their experiences of transnational movement" (Lee, 2016, p. 2586). Moreover, the collaborative aspect of constructing identities has been empowering and transformative, "by choosing to act in culturally appropriate ways they can effectively reclaim their agency, exerting it in ways that gain approval and enable them to develop a new sense of belonging" (pp. 2585–2586) in Toronto urban schools.

Transnational Identity and the politics of belonging

Filipina/o/x youth experiences the affect and the politics of belonging as they navigate their transnational identities. 'Belonging' as a concept is understood as both "personal, intimate, [including] feelings of being 'at home' in a place (place-belongingness) and…a discursive resource that constructs, claims, justifies, or resists forms of socio-spatial inclusion/exclusion (politics of belonging)" (Antonsich, 2010, p. 644). Furthermore, "an analytical differentiation between belonging and the politics of belonging is, therefore, crucial for any critical political discourse on nationalism, racism or other contemporary politics of belonging" (Yuval-Davis, 2006, p. 197). The global migration experiences of Filipina/o/x youth have significantly impacted them on an affective and political level, particularly systemic racism and the impact of colonialism, which they then navigate their transnational identities through their political agency.

Colonization has created hierarchies that have constructed the European colonizer as 'superior', where the colonized have internalized their 'inferiority' (Fanon, 1986). Given the colonial history within the Philippines – mainly by Spain for over 300 years and the United States (McElhinny et al., 2012) as well as Japan (Constantino & Constantino, 1975), the Filipina/o/x community has been constructed through 'Orientalism', "a Western style for dominating restructuring, and having authority over the Orient" (Said, 1979, p. 11). Moreover colonization produced:

> A poverty-breeding society was nurtured, and the widening gap between a wealthy few and the impoverished majority became an apparently insoluble problem. State power was manifested in various ways, all leading to the suppression of any move for basic changes...export crops predominated over produce to feed a grossly expanding population; and the government was burdened with a type of foreign aid which insured that the debtor would be in constant debt to the creditor.
>
> (Constantino & Constantino, 1975, p. 394)

On an individual, collective, and cultural level, Filipina/o/x youth have been impacted by the 'politics of skin colour' and 'colourism' (de Leon, 2012; Pierce, 2005) in their embodied lives, producing a preference of lighter over darker skin colour: "Spain introduced colorism; preferential treatment was clearly associated with lighter skin colo[u]r. Centuries of this education primed the Filipino for vulnerability to internalize American rules of race" (Pierce, 2005, p. 33). Additionally, "the ways in which skin itself is spatial was critical in understanding how the participants' bodies and skins encountered each other in real and imagined ways, as well as how the meaning carried within light or dark skin created particular epidermal boundaries" (de Leon, 2012, p. 398). While the youth experienced racism due to colourism, many of them have resisted these the politics of skin colour through the group art project to challenge the "real and imagined spatial divisions caused by intraracial colourism today. Being open to such dialogue can push against those dominant systems of racial oppression that [these] communities knowingly and unknowingly sustain" (de Leon, 2012, p. 398). The group art project facilitated deeper understandings of how "seemingly instinctive privileging of whiteness within larger, oppressive economic and colonial structures effectively moves the discussion away from the demonization of the colonized, toward more positive strategies for change" (Pierce, 2005, p. 37). School-community partnerships provide this space, in collaboration with Filipina/o/x youth and their mothers as well as Filipina/o/x leaders. Through discussions through the group art projects, critical arts-based inquiry (Finley, 2011) can be seen as a positive strategy where Filipina/o/x youth navigate their individual, cultural, and transnational identities through political agency and in relation to the politics of belonging (Antonsich, 2010; Yuval-Davis, 2006). Through the facilitation of group art projects, school-community partnerships assist Filipina/o/x youth engage in "transformations of [the] self, community, and governance…it is a historical and collective process, and as such, can only be understood within these contexts" (Mohanty, 2003, p. 8).

Racism and navigating transnational identities

Filipina/o/x youth mobilize their experience of systemic racism within the L/CP and in Toronto urban schools through the navigation of their transnational identities and political agency. Eric, 16, indicated that as a transnational student he experienced racism amongst his peers:

Researcher:	Ok, um, so what are your thoughts about how people of different racial backgrounds are treated in your school…do you think racism is happening in schools…?
Eric:	Yeah, maybe. Sometimes they throw comments.
Researcher:	At you or at [other] people?
Eric:	Um, at us.
Researcher:	Like newcomers?
Eric:	Yeah, newcomers.
Researcher:	How about outside in society?…[Have you] experienced racism?
Eric:	No, it didn't happen to me
Researcher:	No, more so in school?
Eric:	In school.

While Eric indicated that he has not experienced racism outside of the school building, educational systems are representative of the systemic racism embedded within society. These particular forms of racism flow through institutions, policies, practices, and society's intersubjective "actions and practices take place in relation to others" (Anthias, 2011, p. 213). Eric navigates these experiences of racism through his political agency as a transnational student and newcomer through an understanding of these intersubjective practices of racism in practice. The racist comments that he and other Filipina/o/x youth experience are mobilized as key tools in coming to deeper understandings of his transnational identity.

Eric's experiences also speaks to the political economy of race embedded within systemic racism, specifically within urban neighbourhoods where people of colour are part of low income households (Anyon, 2013). The urban school that Eric attends is located within the neighbourhoods that consists of "a political economy of race for urban education…when the political economy prevents opportunity for decent jobs and wages in urban areas, and…maintains families in poverty, … [diminishing] the capacity of parents to provide rich, stable learning environments" (Anyon, 2013, p. 369). Eric and his peers face an embodied experience of systemic racism through intersubjective actions and practices such as his peers throwing racist comments toward newcomer and Filipina/o/x transnational students.

The political economy of race (Anyon, 2013) and the intersubjective practices of racism through action and practices (Antonsich, 2010) "emerge in relation to power. This power is both external to the diasporic subject and internally formative" (Cho, 2007, p. 15). Eric demonstrates his political agency as he navigates how systemic racism has impacted his transnational identity and how he makes meaning of identity and belonging in Toronto urban schools.

Additionally, Eric's gendered and sexual identities are "constructed along multiple axes of difference" (Yuval-Davis, 2006, p. 200), intersecting with his racial identity. Identifying as a 'gay' Filipino male who enjoys 'girly-things', he was aware of his sexual and gendered identities since grade 1, understanding that these were markers of difference (Hall, 1997), "I like[d] playing with girls and I don't know why…And I like[d] to play with Barbie things and girly things like that" (Eric, 16). Together, we explored multiple axes of difference, particularly around his gendered & sexual identity:

Researcher: So you identify as boy and gay. In the Philippines, what was your experience like growing up?

Eric: It's very hard because you would be bullied a lot, especially in elementary grade, I've been bullied a lot but in high school…[I] just…ignore[d] the bullying.

Researcher: So it was difficult?

Eric: Yeah, it was difficult [to] be there, but here [in Canada] we just [enjoy] it.

Researcher: Here in Canada…do you find it easier…to [be and say that] you are gay?

Eric: Yeah, it's very welcoming.

Bullying Eric due to his markers of difference (Hall, 1997), specifically his gendered and sexual identities, demonstrates the intersubjective practices and actions (Antonsich,, 2010)

of society, namely through the discriminatory behaviours of his peers toward. It also highlights the power relations in that he learns to engage in political agency (Coloma, 2008) by ignoring the bullying and acknowledging where his gender and sexual identities have been welcome and accepted. Additionally, he navigates the intersection of his markers of difference (Hall, 1997) as a newcomer 'gay' Filipino youth in transnational spaces discrimination and oppression within the Philippines and in Toronto urban schools (Figure 5.1).

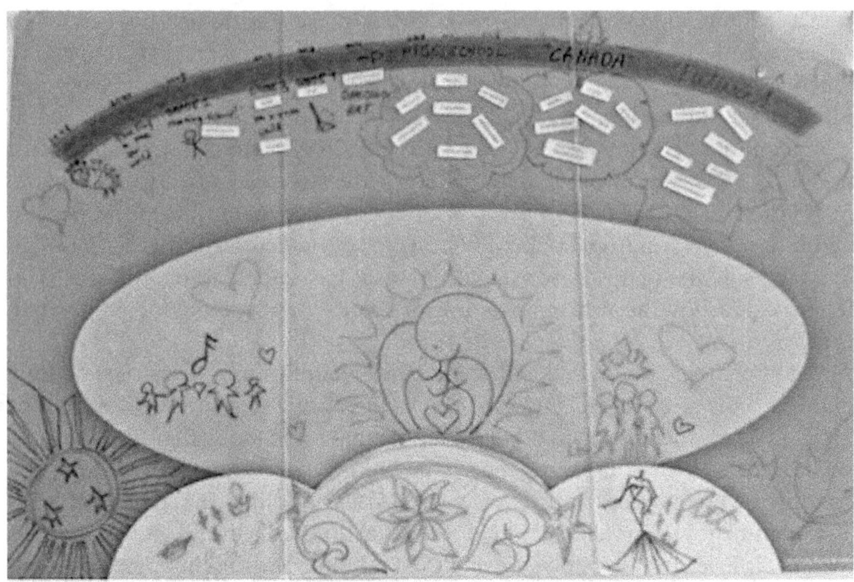

Figure 5.1 Image of Eric's Vidaview Life Story Board (Ticar, 2017)

Ivy (16), Rita (19), and Rachel (18) shared that Philippine society's view of the queer Filipina/o/x community has been influenced by discriminatory perceptions as well as spirituality and religion. Ivy indicated that "usually in the Philippines, when they see gay people or lesbian people, they start to get disgusted or whatever, but in here, I just see people like do whatever". Ivy pinpoints the transnational attitudinal differences between the ways queers are viewed in the Philippines and Canada. While there may be similar feelings within Canada like the Philippines, the power relations appear to be neutral in Canada, according to her viewpoint. Rita observes the 'liberal' behaviours toward queer people in Canada while indicating religious restriction in the Philippines, "I think in the Philippines, they're being judged because more people in the Philippines are based on their religion and like here, they have more freedom". While still identifying as a devout Christian, Rachel engages in political agency as she navigates her transnational religious identity in relation to queerness:

> Growing up…I had friends and family members who were like gay or lesbians…so I just treat them like ["normal people" and] I just see a person…I wasn't allowed to express those thoughts because of strict religious beliefs… I'm not gonna go up to your face and be like oh you're a sinner you're gonna go to hell…yeah, I feel like those Christians who like say that, like, queer people, trans people are, like, not people, I'm like, are you dumb?
>
> (Rachel)

For Rachel, Christianity has been a source of empowerment and identity, nevertheless, she is also able to address the power relations underlying her religious upbringing. She acknowledges the dignity and humanity of the queer community in the Philippines and points out the harmful and oppressive behaviours toward this particular community.

Religion is one of the main remnants of colonization in the Philippines, "the only predominantly Christian country in Asia, a legacy from Roman Catholic Spanish and Protestant American colonizers" (Daly, 2005, p. 228). Rachel's experience of Christianity while growing and Ivy's and Rita's perspectives illuminate "the expression of…sexuality outside prescribed… heterosexist, homophobic norms[,]… [has resulted] in guilt, confusion, and fear" (de Jesús, 2005, p. 9). However, Rachel's political agency in understanding the humanity of the queer community in transnational contexts in the Philippines and in Canada highlights how she "respect[s] tradition even as [she] contest[s] it, disagree[s] with it, and subject[s] it to critique" (Bundang, 2005, p. 67).

The transnational and intersectional identities of Filipina/o/x youth are contingent upon their political agency as well as the power relations embedded within the legacy of colonization. For Philip (16), religion/spirituality is an important part of his transnational identity, despite the legacy of religion through colonialism:

Researcher: Your values, what are [some] important values?
Philip: Godliness.
Researcher: So maybe your spirituality, religion, maybe? What is your religion?
Philip: Catholic.
Researcher: So [being] Catholic is very important to you, going to church and things like that?
Philip: Yes, I go to church but not always.
Researcher: But for you, being spiritual is important?
Philip: Yes, of course Miss.

Philip, through his political agency, makes meaning of his transnational identity and comes to deeper understandings that spirituality is an important value, despite not always going to church.

A significant legacy of colonization within the Philippines is the inability to economically support families and find sustainable employment. Furthermore, this legacy is transnational as the Filipina mothers and their children experience the intersection of class, particularly through low-wage jobs and households. Unanimously, the youth underscored that their mothers had left them to meet their family's economic needs. Eric shared that his mother had to work outside of the Philippines due to economic reasons: "my understanding is that she needs to… sustain our finances…because we are very poor back home, that's why." Rodrigo explained that while his mother had a job in the Philippines, it was not sufficient to raise children and maintain a household. Consequently, his mother moved to Hong Kong and subsequently to Canada as a migrant domestic worker:

Rodrigo: Since my mom had my sister, we couldn't afford anything cause her job was not that good, she was a midwife, and her everyday payment was 200 pesos, I don't know how much it is here, like a few bucks, like 5 bucks a day…so it was really small and she said that she couldn't afford it because my dad doesn't have a permanent job…When I was in grade 4, she was planning to move to Hong Kong.
Researcher: Ah, so she went to Hong Kong first?
Rodrigo: She moved to Hong Kong

Family reunification was prolonged through Rodrigo's mother's move to Hong Kong first before migrating to Canada, a necessarily economic move to ensure the survival of their family. Despite family reunification in Canada, many Filipina mothers worked multiple jobs for survival, a transnational pattern that did not cease after global migration. Filipina mothers maintain their gendered vulnerabilities as low waged workers (Jaggar, 2009) in Canada as these processes are part of the global infrastructure of global cities (Sassen, 2008):

Researcher: So when you moved to Toronto, was it hard for you and your family financially?
Eric: Yeah maybe, like the first month was very hard.
Researcher: Yeah? Um, how about now?
Eric: There's a lot of expenses.
Researcher: Your mom is working many jobs, how many does she have?
Eric: I think she has three jobs.
Researcher: She has three jobs?!
Eric: Yeah.

Rodrigo's and Eric's global migration stories through the L/CP construct "the inclusion or exclusion of particular people…politics involves the exercise of power and [the] different hegemonic political projects of belonging represent different symbolic power orders" (Yuval-Davis, 2011, pp. 18–19). Despite 'belonging' as a Permanent Residents in Canada, Rodrigo, Eric, and their mothers still experience low economic stability, where they experience exclusion from access to necessary resources.

Group Art Projects

Through the Group Art Projects, Filipina/o/x youth navigated their transnational identities, which took place at *Services for a Diverse Community* (SDC) and the *Newcomer Support Centre* (NSC). The group art projects were adapted from

Taylor and Murphy's (2013) '*Paper Quilt*', a collective art project includes each participant to provide their individual piece on a banner to that represents their cultural identity. The first two groups were from SDC and the third was from the NSC. Each 2 hour session consisted of a group discussion around how they mobilized the traumas of family separation and reunification in Toronto urban schools individually through the Vidaview Life Storyboard (Chase et al., 2012). The first group art session consisted of about 10 participants where it was mainly silent and the Filipina/o/x youth appeared to be shy. As the facilitator, I attempted to connected with them in a culturally-relevant way and said "for me, food seemed to be an important part of the sessions." Subsequently, some of the youth nodded and seemingly had relieving laughter and shy giggles afterwards. Then I asked how it was like to reunify with their mothers. One student answered "We got used to being without her so being distant with her is normal". For some of the youth, their entry point in connecting with their peers was to express the entanglements of family separation and reunification as a tool to make meaning of their transnational identities.

I then asked who are the Filipina/o/x youth missing in the Philippines. They mentioned grandparents and extended family members such as aunts, uncles, and cousins. I kept the conversation short as I was aware that these particular youth had recently reunified with their mothers. After the group conversation, they dispersed to their tables in smaller groups and then drew and/or wrote symbols about their meaningful memories on a piece of paper for their individual part of the group art project. In silence and reflection, they seemed more comfortable and engaged with this process. At the end of the project, they drew significant cultural symbols such as fiestas of the particular regions they identified with; crosses to symbolize their faith, flags such as the Philippines and Canada; airplanes to symbolize their migration experiences; and hearts to represent what is important to them (Figure 5.2).

Figure 5.2 Image of Group Art Project (Ticar, 2017)

The next group art project seemed to be more relaxed as there were only three students who participated. Additionally, it may have had to do with the fact that the two newcomer students did not experience family separation and reunification through the L/CP. The students spoke and laughed about their school experiences about being newcomers, having been in Toronto for over a year. While the first group had only lived in Toronto for under 6 months and were still getting to know some of the other Filipina/o/x youth, the youth in the second group were also close friends who spoke about teachers and talked about being newcomers as the 'past' rather than being in the present. They drew pictures of political figures, family, and favourite memories of the Philippines, which they 'miss'. These memories are a "process of intense discovery and disorientation… it is such a memory of the history of race and racism, and the question of cultural identity" (Bhabha, 1994, p. 63). The second group navigated their experiences as newcomers and were building strong individual and collective transnational identities while building community with one another.

The third group consisted of three Filipino boys who are close friends at the SDC. They attend the same school and have been in Toronto for over a year. They spoke of the romantic relationships left behind in the Philippines and having a complete 'heart' after family reunification. Leaving behind relationships through global migration can be heartbreaking, "remembering is never a quiet act of introspection or retrospection. It is painful remembering, a putting together of the dismembered past to make sense of the trauma of the present" (Bhabha, 1994, p. 63). Much like the second group art project, the youth have already built a sense of community with one another and have been in Toronto over a year. Each of these boys had experienced family separation and reunification, and unlike the first group, they had strong bonds with their mothers. This may have been an effect of being reunified for a longer duration in comparison to the first group who were relatively new in Toronto urban schools.

For all of the students in each of the group art projects, the Philippines and their families are important aspects of their memories and migration trajectories. Many of the students value community and described missing 'fiestas,' events that kept their communities lively. These artworks embody the complexity of the youths' lives as they have 'pieces' of themselves here and in the Philippines as well as other places in the world. Memories and emotions serve as a connection to their loved ones left behind in the Philippines, and I was a "witness to the unequal and uneven… political[,]…social[,] [and cultural]" forces (Bhabha, 1994, p. 171)" that Filipina/o/x youth and their mothers face during their global migration experiences through the L/CP. Through the group art projects, Filipina/o/x youth make meaning of transnational identity and belonging in Toronto urban schools in community with their peers.

While a few of the youth did not experience family separation through the L/CP, and neither have I, we were co-performers who provided community support through the facilitation of school-community partnerships and Filipina/o/x community leaders. The group art projects were a cultural performance, "a lens for examining culture, particularly the communication practices of subaltern groups – the power of symbols and imagination in both consolidating and contesting oppression and how cultural creativity and human agency are both inscribed and incited by domination" (Johnson, 2013, p. 7). Thus, the symbols of flags; reuniting with family members; food; fiestas; religion; and other symbols of their transnational imagination are the agentic ways in which they make meaning of their identity and belonging in Toronto urban schools.

Conclusion

In this chapter, I attempted to provide a cultural representation of transnational youth's experiences of global migration through the L/CP. The SDC and the NSC were the sites in which transnational feminist praxis took place through school-community partnerships. The group art workshop further helped to crystallize (Ellingson, 2011) a system of cultural representation "a process, a set of *practices* [which are] concerned with the production and the exchange of meanings… between members of a society or group" (Hall, 1996, p. 2). Whether the youth newly arrived or have been in Toronto urban schools for over a year, they made meaning of their transnational identity and belonging through community. The crystallized representation (Ellingson, 2011) through the group art projects synthesized oral history and memory methods as well as critical arts-based inquiry (Finley, 2011) to understand the Filipina/o/x youths' transnational identity and the politics of belonging (Antonsich, 2010; Yuval-Davis, 2006) in Toronto urban schools, providing further insight into their agency under transnational conditions of family separation and reunification. Thus, "critical arts-based inquiry…is both a mode of inquiry and a methodology for performing social activism" (Finley, 2011, p. 436). Paying attention to the youth's emotions and visual representations of those affective responses in conjunction with a triangulated account of community leaders and the parents themselves revealed a lot, sometimes more than words, and conveyed a very powerful message: "Family separation and reunification hurts me, my family, and my community. What are you going do about it?"

Note

1 All the names of the participants in this chapter have been changed to pseudonyms

References

Anthias, F. (2011). Intersections and translocations: New paradigms for thinking about cultural diversity and social identities. *European Educational Research Journal*, *10*(2), 204–217.

Antonsich, M. (2010). Searching for belonging: An analytical framework. *Geography Compass*, *4*(6), 644–659.

Anyon, J. A. (2013). Political economy of race, urban education, and educational policy. In C. McCarthy, W. Crichlow, G. Dimitriadis, & N. Dolby (Eds.), *Race, identity, and representation in education*, (2nd ed.) (pp. 369–378).

Bhabha, H. K. (1994). *The location of culture*. Routledge.

Bhuyan, R., Valmadrid, L., Panlaqui, E. L., Pendon, N. L., & Juan, P. (2018). Responding to the structural violence of migrant domestic work: Insights from participatory action research with migrant caregivers in Canada. *Journal of Family Violence*, *33*(8), 613–627. https://doi.org/10.1007/s10896-018-9988-x

Bundang, R. A. R. (2005). This is not your mother's catholic church: When Filipino catholic spirituality meets American culture. In M. L. de Jesús (Ed.), *Pinay power: Peminist critical theory: Theorizing the Filipina/American experience* (pp. 61–80). Routledge.

Chase, R.M., Medina, M.F. & Mignone, J. (2012). The life story board: A feasibility study of a visual interview tool for school counsellors. *Canadian Journal of Counselling and Psychotherapy/Revue canadienne de counseling et de psychothérapie* 46(3), 183–200.

Cho, L. (2007). The turn to diaspora. *TOPIA*,17.

Coloma, R. S. (2008). Border crossing subjectivities and research: Through the prism of feminists of color. *Race, Ethnicity, and Education*, *11*(1), 11–27.

Constantino, R., & Constantino, L. R. (1975). *A history of the Philippines: From the Spanish colonization to the second world war*. Monthly Review Press.

Daly, P. P. (2005). Creating NewFilipina.Com and the rise of CyberPinays. In M. L. de Jesús (Ed.), *Pinay power: Peminist critical theory: Theorizing the Filipina/American experience* (pp. 221–238). Routledge.

de Jesús, M. L. (2005). *Pinay power: Peminist critical theory: Theorizing the Filipina/American experience*. Routledge.

de Leon, C. (2012). Mas maputi ko sa 'yo (I'm lighter than you): The spatial politics of intraracial colourism among Filipina/o youth in the greater Toronto area. In R. S. Coloma, B. McElhinny, E. Tungohan, J. P. C. Cantugal, & L. M. Davidson (Eds.), *Filipinos in Canada: Disturbing invisibility* (pp. 382–401). University of Toronto Press.

Dreby, J. (2007). Children and power in Mexican transnational families. *Journal of Marriage and Family*, *69*(4), 1050–1064. http://www.jstor.org.proxy1.lib.uwo.ca/stable/4622507.

Ellingson, L. L. (2011). Analysis and representation across the continuum. In N. K. Denzin, & Y. S. Lincoln (Eds.), *SAGE handbook of qualitative research* (pp. 595–610). SAGE.

Eyerman, R. (2019). *Memory, trauma, and identity*. Palgrave Macmillan.

Fanon, F. (1986). *Black skin, white masks* (C.L. Markmann, Trans.). Pluto Press. (Original work published 1952).

Finley, S. (2011). Critical arts-based inquiry: The pedagogy and performance of a radical ethical aesthetic. In N. Denzin, & Y. Lincoln (Eds.), *The SAGE handbook of qualitative research* (pp. 435–450). SAGE.

Goodman, D. J., & Jackson, B. W. III (2012). Pedagogical approaches to teaching about racial identity from an intersectional perspective. In C. L. Wijeyesinghe, & B. W. Jackson (Eds.), *New perspectives on racial identity development: Integrating emerging frameworks* ((2nd ed) ed., pp. 216–240). New York University Press.

Hall, S. (1996). *Questions of cultural identity*. SAGE. https://web-p-ebscohost-com.library.smu.ca/ehost/detail/detail?vid=0&sid=c6cc466d-3d7b-4678-ab0e-c7ac0e06a92a%40redis&bdata=JnNpdGU9ZWhvc3QtbGl2ZQ%3d%3d#AN=716879&db=e000xna

Hall, S. (1997). *Representation: Cultural representations and signifying practices*. SAGE.

Hoang, L. A., & Yeoh, B. S. A. (2015). Children's agency and its contradictions in the context of transnational labour migration from Vietnam. *Global Networks*, *15*(2), 180–197. doi: 10.1111/glob.12057.

Hörschelmann, K., & El Refaie, E. (2014). Transnational citizenship, dissent and the political geographies of youth. *Transactions of the Institute of British Geographers, 39*(3), 444–456. doi: 10.1111/tran.12033.

Jaggar, A. M. (2009). Transnational cycles of gendered vulnerability: A prologue to the theory of global gender justice. *Philosophical Topics*, 33–52.

Johnson, E. P. (2013). Introduction: 'Opening and interpreting lives'. In E. P. Johnson (Ed.), *Cultural struggles: Performance, ethnography, praxis* (pp. 1–14). University of Michigan.

Lee, H. (2016). 'I was forced here': Perceptions of agency in second generation 'return' migration to Tonga. *Journal of Ethnic and Migration Studies, 42*(15), 2573–2588. doi: 10.1080/1369183X.2016.1176524.

McCall, L. (2005). The complexity of intersectionality. *Journal of Women in Culture and Society, 30*(3), 1771–1880.

McElhinny, B., Davidson, L. M., Cantugal, J. P. C., Tungohan, E., & Coloma, R. S. (2012) Spectres of (in)visibility: Filipina/o labour, culture and youth in Canada. In R.S. Coloma., B. McElhinny, E. Tungohan, J.P.C. Cantugal & L.M Davidson (Eds.), *Filipinos in Canada: Disturbing invisibility* (pp. 5–45). University of Toronto Press.

Mohanty, C. T. (2003). *Feminism without borders: Decolonizing theory, practicing solidarity*. Duke University Press.

Mohapatra, A. K. (2006). The paradox of return: Origins, home and identity in M.G. Vassanji's *The Gunny Sack. Postcolonial Text, 2*(4), 1–21.

Nagar, R., & Swarr, A. L. (2010). *Critical transnational feminist praxis*. SUNY Press. https://library.smu.ca/login?url=https://search.ebscohost.com/login.aspx?direct=true&db=e000xna&AN=306680&site=ehost-live

Pierce, L. M. (2005). Not just my closet: Exposing familial, cultural, and imperial skeletons. In M. L. de Jesús (Ed.), *Pinay power: Peminist critical theory: Theorizing the Filipina/American experience* (pp. 31–44). Routledge.

Pratt, G. (2012). *Families apart: Migrant mothers and conflicts of labour and love*. University of Minnesota Press.

Said, E. W. (1979). *Orientalism* (1st vintage books ed.). Vintage Books.

Sassen, S. (2008). Two stops in today's new global geographies: Shaping novel labour supplies and employment regimes. *American Behavioral Scientist, 52*(3), 457–496.

Taylor, P., & Murphy, C. (2013). *Catch the fire: An art-full guide to unleashing the creative power of youth, adults and communities*. New Society Publishers.

Ticar, J. E. (2017). *Investigating the transnational identities of Filipina/o/x youth in Toronto urban high schools: A critical ethnographic study of the impact of Canada's Live-In/Caregiver Program*. ProQuest Dissertations & Theses.

Tungohan, E. (2012). Debunking notions of migrant 'Victimhood': A critical assessment of temporary labour migration programs and Filipina migrant activism in Canada. In R.S. Coloma., B. McElhinny, E. Tungohan, J.P.C. Catungal & L.M Davidson (Eds.), *Filipinos in Canada: Disturbing invisibility* (pp. 161–80), University of Toronto.

Voicu, C.-G. (2014). *Exploring cultural identities in jean Rhys' fiction*. De Gruyter.

Youkhana, E. (2015). A conceptual shift in studies of belonging and the politics of belonging. *Social Inclusion, 3*(4), 10–24.

Yuval-Davis, N. (2006). Belonging and the politics of belonging. *Patterns of Prejudice, 40*(3), 197–214.

Yuval-Davis, N. (2011). *The politics of belonging: Intersectional contestations*. SAGE.

Yuval-Davis, N. (2012, January 27). An Intersectional Gaze at Nationalist Projects: Women and Men of Particular Contexts [Video File]. https://youtu.be/OiOAdou8B9o.

6 Making meaning of critical social justice

Introduction

> When I learned about [Indigenous] peoples], I realized we should take action, cause, you know, if we keep on being silent…we shouldn't expect change.
>
> (Angelica)

In the previous chapter I discussed how Filipina/o/x youth navigate their intersectional and transnational identities in Toronto urban schools through school-community partnerships. This chapter draws upon the narratives of Filipina/o/x youth and community leaders to come to deeper understandings of how school-community partnerships address the impact of settler colonialism through decolonization and solidarities within Indigenous-settler-migrant relations. School-community partnerships engaged in transnational feminist praxis (Nagar & Swarr, 2010) through its facilitation of the "collective practice of [transforming] the self, [the] reconceptualization of identity, and political mobilization" (Mohanty, 2003, p. 8).

Facing colonial domination, anti-blackness, and queer erasure

School-community partnerships had provided Alicia, an 18-year-old Filipina, transformative space to unpack anti-Black racism that she heard within the Filipina/o/x community in the Philippines and in Canada by challenging the notion that Blackness was associated with being 'bad':

> There was something that most people tell me and sometimes my mom right now, in the present, my mom kind of goes into…like how people with dark skin can be considered 'bad' I guess? Like, cause you know how back home, like, they consider the idea of a Black person as bad, I don't know why, it's probably because of the colour, like Black, white, stuff like that, so my mom probably has issues with Black people cause of how they act. Like, sometimes I hear stories from her about how Black people are 'violent.' And I don't think that.
>
> (Alicia)

DOI: 10.4324/9781003287469-6

Here, Alicia negotiated colonial ideas that have been passed down from generation to generation, but is able to challenge them in a way such that these ideas are not internalized and reproduced. She was able to point out the connection between skin colour and racism and decide for herself that she does not agree with the oppressive ideology that 'Black people are bad.' Alicia's personal experience with racism was on an intersubjective level as it was not directed towards her as an individual but on the level of concrete social relations and systemic oppression on the basis of race (Anthias, 2011). She utilized her political agency to resist and work towards dismantling anti-Black racism through her participation in school-community partnerships programs.

Additionally, the domination of whiteness within the West speaks to the global power relations stemming from colonialism, and white privilege on a global level (Pierce, 2005). Within this structure of colonization in West, those who are not constructed as 'white' are seen as the 'Other', "Orientalism can be discussed and analyzed as the corporate institution for dealing with the Orient… by making statements about it, authorizing views of it, describing it, by teaching it, settling it, ruling over it" (p. 11). These processes of 'orientalism' are seen within Toronto urban schools where racist spaces are evident. According to Angelica, her early days of schooling were quite difficult:

> I didn't know anything, my first day was a mess, like, yeah I didn't know anything, I was shocked when the bell rang cause I didn't know what was happening, why is everyone standing? Where [are] they going?… I even experienced crying in the washroom…Like during lunch, like I always feel like I'm alone cause I don't know it's different cause I was shocked with the diversity. I was expecting, like I'm not racist, but I was expecting like America is white people, like I don't know…I didn't know that Canada will be so diverse…Cause, if you go to the Philippines and you say Americans, they're gonna expect like white people.
>
> (Angelica)

Additionally, as a transnational newcomer student, Angelica had experienced discrimination from Filipina/o/x youth and other youth of colour who have been in Canada longer than her:

> Here in Toronto, yeah, like I remember during my first days here at [school], um, some of the Filipinos that have been here for a while, they're kind of bullies and some of the other cultures, they call us like FOBS [Fresh off the Boat]. There's a part in the cafe where all of the new Filipinos sit, I don't know cause all of the new Filipinos are really not used to speaking in English, so everyone is going to come together cause all of them speak Tagalog, right? And some of the Black people are going to be like 'FOBS'.
>
> (Angelica)

Intergenerational discrimination occurs when the Filipina/o/x community has "internalized the anti-Asian and anti-immigrant rhetoric and practices that characterize so much of the culture and social structure…some Filipinos adopt anti-black and anti-Latino racism in an effort to secure ethnic inclusion for themselves" (Espiritu, 2003, pp. 142–143). This is when 'inclusion' becomes dangerous as it then simply constitutes a move towards the norm of whiteness and reproduces white supremacy.

Eric reported similar concerns like Angelica around comments being thrown in the cafeteria where newcomer Filipina/o/x students congregate and speak with each other in Tagalog and other Philippine languages and dialects. The term 'FOB' symbolizes a marker of difference in which newcomer youth have been excluded. Angelica's and Eric's lived experience as racialized and newcomer youth facing racism is a manifestation of "multiple intersecting inequalities" (Anthias, 2011, p. 3) in Toronto urban school where, "social division[s] interrelate in terms of the production of social relations, and in terms of people's lives" (Anthias, 2011, p. 4).

Gender and sexuality, particularly when it comes to queerness, are also intersections that reproduce power relations within the Filipina/o/x community. Darlene, a Filipina community leader who identifies as a lesbian, assists transnational Filipina mothers relate with their children, especially when it comes queer Filipina/o/x children and/or mothers 'coming out'. Darlene acknowledges the intersections between race, gender, sexuality, religion, and spirituality and its complications and nuances within the context of culturally-relevant interventions:

> It would be good to do stuff on sex education too, in the context of a highly Catholic culture, that's respectful, right? Or family traditions or family values, everyone has a sexuality, everyone has questions, how might parents be supported, in their own kind of way, because I think there's a lot of services for queer youth, and there's less services for culturally-specific queer youth, but what about the parents? The parents kind of want to have their own supports. When I came out, my mom thought I would be the only gay Filipino in the world and because she didn't know any other parents. Right? So, a safe place for them to kind of ask support, meet folks, dispel some myths, and something intergenerational.
>
> (Darlene)

Darlene's intersectional approach towards working with transnational Filipina/o/x families acknowledges the need for culturally-relevant services for queer youth and parents that use intergenerational knowledge(s) that have implications for school-community partnerships.

This intersectional approach that Darlene posits provides space for school-community partnerships to engage in transnational feminist praxis (Nagar & Swarr, 2010) so that Filipina/o/x youth like Eric, a Filipino youth we meet in chapter 5, engage in their political agency when constructing their intersectional identities, specifically gender and sexuality in relation to race. Darlene provides key information regarding social service provision for transnational Filipina/o/x families, particularly with those who identify 'queer'. School-community partnerships highlight the importance of sharing stories and providing community support, engaging in transnational feminist praxis (Nagar & Swarr, 2010) as they provide space for transnational Filipina/o/x families to utilize their political agency. Moreover, school-community partnerships are a site in which Filipina/o/x community leaders "must… also learn from their students. The differences and borders of each of our identities connect us to each other, more than they sever" (Mohanty, 2003, pp. 250–251).

School-community partnerships and solidarities

School-community partnerships are also a site of building solidarities among transnational students such as Filipina/o/x youth and Indigenous communities, creating safe spaces and learning opportunities. In turn, the leaders of these institutions may provide the space to build solidarities without "obliterating difference" (Hall, 1996, p. 3) between different communities. Furthermore, this chapter examines that situated context of settler colonialism in Canada and the role of racialized communities in dismantling the continual colonization of Indigenous peoples in Canada (Mahtini & Roberts, 2012). I posit that school-community partnerships play a significant role in dismantling settler colonialism and the impact of colonization on Indigenous Nations, specifically within educational policies and practices that go beyond the classroom. Moreover, this chapter examines how school-community partnerships have been significant spaces in which to embody transnational feminist praxis, highlighting Filipina/o/x youths' individual and collective agency and perspectives on solidarities with Indigenous Nations.

This chapter includes perspectives of Filipina/o/x community leaders, two from NSC and seven from SDC. There is a wide range of experience of these leaders working in school-community partnerships, from 3 months to 27.5 years, in various roles. These community leaders also work with Filipina mothers and some have worked with both Filipina/o/x families.

Table 6.1 Filipina/o/x community leaders (Ticar, 2017)

Pseudonym	*Site/partnership*	*Role in site*	*Years of experience*
Carla	SDC	Partner, educational consultant	8 years
Catherine	SDC	School settlement worker/program co-ordinator	3 years
Cynthia	SDC	Partner/school social worker	3 months
Darlene	SDC	Partner/community arts educator	4 years
Nora	SDC	School settlement worker	6 months
Selma	NSC	Settlement worker	26 years
Silvana	SDC	Partner, community arts educator	6 years
Sonya	NSC	Executive Director	27.5 years
Valerie	SDC	School settlement worker	6 years

Perspectives of Filipina/o/x youth on solidarities

At the time of our interview in 2016, Angelica was 17 years old. She had identified as a 'shy' Filipina who did not speak 'English well'. However, during our conversation, she seemed outgoing, expressive, and engaging, speaking English fluently. She exuded student leadership qualities as she seemed to give advice to the newcomer youth to help with their adjustment in Toronto urban schools. She shared that upon arriving to Canada in 2015, she learned about many aspects of settler colonialism through the school curriculum and in after school programs with Filipina/o/x community leaders. She highlighted that at her school, students have been learning about the colonial histories of Indigenous Nations and in attempts to engage in decolonization and solidarities, students have been connected with Elders in these communities to learn about their cultures and histories. Many of the transnational students at Angelica's school had migrated from various countries of Africa, the Caribbean, and Latin America as well as from Iraq, Syria, and the Philippines.

School-community partnerships had played a significant role in decolonization and facilitating deeper understandings of the ongoing settler colonialism in Canada. Angelica appreciates learning about the situation of Indigenous peoples; otherwise, she indicated that she 'would not have cared' about justice for Indigenous Nations. Voicing the need to be aware of the genocidal histories Indigenous peoples is twofold in that school-community partnerships attempt to build solidarities between transnational students and they illuminate the need for decolonization, giving 'land back' to Indigenous Nations and centring Indigenous Sovereignty (Tuck & Yang, 2012). With regards to the Black communities and Indigenous peoples in Canada, Amadhy and Lawrence (2009) who spoke to the relations between Black migrants and Indigenous peoples in Canada:

> The strength of the historic connections between Black and Native people has been weakened by exclusionary racial classification, by anti-Black racism among Native people and a profound ignorance on the part of many contemporary Black people about Indigenous presence, nevertheless, it appears that there will be growing movements of Black-Native people across both Canada and the United States to reclaim indigeneity – not only to lost African roots but to contemporary Native realities in Canada.
>
> (p. 126)

This has implications for school-community partnerships and their responsibilities in educating youth about the ongoing settler colonialism impacting Indigenous Nations as well as in building solidarities among marginalized communities such as dismantling anti-Black racism.

At the beginning of this chapter, Angelica states, "When I learned about [Indigenous] peops], I realized we should take action, cause, you know, if we keep on being silent...we shouldn't expect change" (Angelica). Angelica demonstrates political agency in collaboration with school-community partnerships as she comes to deeper understanding(s) that critical social justice involves action.

Critical social justice

School-community partnerships have a community organizing role when working with transnational Filipina/o/x families, intervening in the "white heteropatriarchal logics enmeshed in the settler colonial project of Canada" (p. 60) that has impacted Filipina/o/x communities (Farrales, 2019). Transnational feminist praxes are one of the ways in which to engage with transnational Filipina/o/x youth and their mothers, providing entry points for deeper understandings of "the multiple ways in which [to] (re)structure colonial and neocolonial relations of domination and subordination" (Nagar & Swarr, 2010, p. 5)", where school-community partnerships attend to the situated and global powers impacting particular communities, such as the Filipina/o/x community in Toronto.

While school-community partnerships still have a way to go in moving towards 'land back' (Tuck & Yang (2009), they are making small progressive steps to "disrupt, subvert, or sabotage the structures of our institutions through acts of radical solidarity [and] foreclose coalition…and the possibility of a present and future that makes space for Blackness and Indigeneity…in conversation with one another [so] that we can make this future we desire" (Curley et al, 2022, p. 1058). Tuck (2009) proposes that a 'desire-based' future looks at futures of Indigenous communities and posits that they are more than the damage that they continually experience. While the experiences of marginalized groups are incommensurable, social justice looks different for different communities (Tuck & Yang, 2012; 2021). Nevertheless, solidarities and decolonization are possible (Curley et al., 2022). One of the ways Indigenous Sovereignty could look like is for Indigenous Nations to have a decision-making role in im/migration policy and practices in Canada (Bauder & Breen, 2022).

According to Rachel, she found that history classes were 'one-sided' and expressed disappointment with the current curriculum as it is. It speaks to how to individualistic the approach is to address the ongoing colonialism rather than systemic efforts at the time of the interviews in 2016. Rachel, an 18-year old Filipina who came to Toronto in 2015, was a student at a different school board from Angelica. She expressed her frustration with not learning about Indigenous people in the curriculum, but through people in her community:

> They shouldn't limit what we can learn, you know?…In history, it was all about war….It was only about what Canada played in the war….And so you don't really get the other side of the story…So you think Canada is this, but what if they're wrong? What if there's another story involved?… I mean you're in Canada but you shouldn't just focus on Canada cause

> I don't know, here, when I found out about Indigenous people, I kind of hated Canada for a while, because I'm like what?! And I thought you guys were so friendly and kind!!!
>
> (Rachel)

This unveiling of the 'truth' is palpable. Fed with hegemonic ideals of Canada being a place of diversity and multiculturalism, Rachel was hit with the truth and upset at the fact that her educational institution hid the occurrence of residential schooling, like a 'dirty little secret'. It also illuminates how residential school was hidden from mainstream society prior to the findings of the mass grave sites of residential school students in 2021. Rachel's expression of 'hatred' and exclusion of Indigenous lives from the curriculum is indicative of the erasure of Indigenous voices and lives within mainstream society. This 'hatred' can also be mobilized to explore 'subversive possibilities' and an "un-doing [of] existing educational policies and practices that exclude and marginalise migrant children" (Zembylas, 2012, p. 173) and Indigenous Nations. Here I connect power relations, emotion, and the ways in which "discourses about migrants and their families [reveal] the structures of feeling that are created by educational policies and practices to maintain particular forms of relationality that contribute to the formation of certain inclusions/exclusions" (p. 172). The emotional economies of migrants have an impact on educational institutions as emotions speak to who is included/excluded when defining one's identity and belonging (Zembylas, 2012). Thus, policy makers and educators "can benefit from interrogating the normative politics of emotions about migrants and [Indigenous Nations] and constantly [question] how particular emotion discourses and practices are embodied in the day-to-day routines of schools and higher education institutions" (Zembylas, 2012, p. 173).

Embodied affect and praxis

School-community partnerships highlight the importance of critical emotional praxis, which is "informed by emotion that resists unjust systems and practices as well as emotion that helps create a more fair and just world in our classrooms and our everyday lives... [and] cope with the social, cultural and political structures in their work (Zembylas, 2012, p. 174). How does critical emotional praxis (Zembylas, 2012), if possible, translate to Indigenous relations on a transnational level? Investigating emotions is the transaction "between macro-political aspects and the micro-politics of local realities" (Zembylas, 2012, p. 175). On a micro-level, listening to students' perspectives and emotions could help improve pedagogy and curriculum, particularly with regards to building relevant connections and productive and nurturing relationships (Zembylas, 2012) among transnational youth and Indigenous Nations in Canada. On a global level, "global movements of Indigenous people, or of 'first nations' have grown out of resistance movements...of various European Settler Societies...all have suffered discrimination, inferiorization, displacement and dispossession to varying degrees" (Yuval-Davis, 2011, p. 103). While each context is different, the connecting point is that Indigenous and transnational migrant movements have grown out of 'resistance'. In the Canadian context, Lawrence and Dua (2005) identify an ongoing point of contention: people of colour as settlers despite experiencing forms of oppression such as racism as they continue to be complicit with the forms of settler colonialism evident in Canada, not engaging in decolonization centring Indigenous Sovereignty (Tuck & Yang, 2012). Mahtini and Roberts (2012) take up this question as well as the social positioning of the Filipina/o/x, im/migrants and Canadians alike, and the:

> Ongoing colonialism of Canada as a white settler society. What might be Filipina/o[/x] Canadians' role in dismantling ongoing racial violence in the lives of [Indigenous] peoples in Canada? How can Filipina/o[/x] Canadians, given their complex transnational role and relationships with other colonizing societies, such as Spain and the United States, understand their relationships with Canadian First Nations? How might this complicate the types of activism and thinking around social justice that would likely form the basis of a way forward or next step with this analysis? How can Filipina/o[/x] Canadians integrate understandings of the Canadian state as a white settler nation into their conceptions of identity?
> (p. 425)

This is where transnational feminist praxis and critical emotional praxis could grow in terms of addressing ongoing settler colonial Canadian society. Given that Filipina/o/x communities for centuries have been subjugated colonial subjects of Spain, Japan, and the United States, provides context for internalized racism and the adoption of colonial and settler colonial values to assimilate, for example, the 'model minority' mindset that renders one in closer proximity to whiteness. The marginalized position of the Filipina/o/x community makes it difficult to challenge and speak back to oppressive structures, and often the choice for some racialized communities is to assimilate for survival. However, Filipina/o/x youth, in collaboration with their mothers and school-community partnerships have been challenging and 'resisting' colonial mentality, particularly around skin colour and standards of beauty, dismantling settler colonialism through their connection with Indigenous Elders, and challenging anti-Black racism. It speaks to how dismantling settler colonialism and colonial mentality are nearly impossible through individual efforts; critical social justice needs to be systemic, organized through a collective ethic of care that involves moves towards decolonization as well as transnational and critical emotional praxes. Thus, educational systems are considered institutions where these questions can possibly be addressed through "collaborative prax[e]s... can become a rich source of methodological *and* theoretical interventions and agendas that can begin the process of identifying and re/claiming those spaces" (Nagar & Swarr, 2010, p. 9).

Filipina/o/x youth and community leaders and Filipina mothers on educators

School-community partnerships may be utilized as a decolonization tool or a tool to reproduce colonial power relations. When it comes to Filipina/o/x teachers and 're/claiming' space within the educational system, Filipina/o/x youth and mothers have had diverse perspectives:

Researcher: If you had a Filipina or Filipino teacher as a role model, would that be helpful for you?
Edna: In here?
Researcher: Yeah if you had a Filipino teacher…does it matter?
Edna: I don't think it matters.
Researcher: As long as they help you adjust?
Edna: Yeah.

Angelica also agreed that having a Filipina/o/x teacher as a role model is unnecessary and shared her perspective:

Angelica: An excellent teacher would be the one who would be strict but know[s] her limits, and [an] excellent teacher…should know what she is doing.
Researcher: Would [it] make a difference if you had a Filipina or Filipino teacher, or does it matter if they're good? So does race matter in terms of being a good teacher? What do you think?
Angelica: No, not really. Well, cause, it really depends on how she or he delivers the lessons because teachers, you know, have different kinds of styles and way of teaching.

However, some of the youth preferred to have Filipina/o/x teachers as a role model, particularly in relating to them on a cultural level and connecting through language:

Researcher: So what are your thoughts about having a Filipina or Filipino teacher as a role model? Like, does [it] matter if the teacher is Filipino?
Eric: I think it matters.
Researcher: It would help with your adjustment?
Eric: Yeah, adjustment.

Cara's perspective also resonated with Eric's:

Researcher: What are your thoughts about having a Filipina or Filipino teacher as a role model?

Cara: Yeah it can help me a lot cause I rarely speak English so she can help me adjust to the language.

Interestingly, the parents did not think that having a Filipina/o/x teacher would make a difference, except for one, Angelica's mother, Natalia, who indicated that, "Yes, Filipina teachers know how to make their students fear them and do their work. Being too strict is bad, but it does help." Natalia's perspective implies that using 'fear' is an effective strategy that 'Canadian' educators may not possess in relation to their Filipina/o/x counterparts. The legacy of US colonialism is its educational system, where the Philippines is the site of subjugation:

> The most effective means of subjugating a people is to capture their minds. Military victory does not necessarily signify conquest…The molding of men's minds is the best means of conquest. Education, therefore, serves as weapon in wars of colonial conquest…The primary reason for the rapid introduction, on a large scale, of the American public school system in the Philippines was the conviction of the military leaders that no measure could so quickly promote the pacification of the islands as education.
>
> (Constantino, 1966, p. 2)

The domination of heteropatriarchy and colonialism is embedded within the US educational system, which some Filipina mothers and their children uphold as they migrate to Canada. This sort of imperialist domination caused fear among those subjugated to colonial rule, introducing hierarchies within the educational system: "Under previous colonial regimes, education saw to it that the Filipino mind was taught to view them objectively, seeing their virtues as well as their faults. This led out citizens to form a distorted opinion of the foreign masters and also of themselves" (Constantino, 1966, p. 16).

This fear tactic also seems to play out in Emilia's, Eric's mother's statement, "I prefer [a] Canadian teacher because I want to improve my [child's] English." For Emilia, speaking English seems to be a marker of success for Eric, and possibly, moving closer in proximity to whiteness within a settler colonial society such as Canada. Hall (1997) argues that through an 'integrationist strategy', "Blacks could gain entry to the mainstream – but only at the cost of adapting to the white image of them and assimilating white norms of style, looks and behaviour" (p. 270). Emilia seems to have adopted to the 'assimilationist' ideal so that her son, Eric, whom she has high hopes and dreams for, would be successful in mainstream society. Moreover, it is intertwined with her own hopes and dreams for her child's future and his success that is embedded within systemic oppression and racism. Implicit in Emilia's statement is the internalization of the superiority of Western culture, specifically with regard to language stemming to US colonialism, as Constantino (1966) argued:

> The first and perhaps the master stroke in the plan to use education as an instrument of colonial policy was the decision to use English as the medium of instruction. English became the wedge that separated the Filipinos from their past and later to separate educated Filipinos from the masses of their countrymen. English introduced the Filipinos to a strange, new world. With American textbooks, Filipinos started learning not only a new language but also a new way of life, alien to their traditions and yet a caricature of their model. This was the beginning of their education. At the same time, it was the beginning of their mis-education, for they learned no longer as Filipinos but as colonials.
>
> (p. 5)

Evelyn, a mother who came through the L/CP, shared that having a Filipina/o/x 1:1 tutor may be helpful in terms of the language and cultural adjustment, but believes that her children do not necessarily need to have a Filipina/o/x teacher. All the community leaders agreed that having a Filipina/o/x teacher would make a significant difference, particularly in terms of cultural representation of teachers within the school system, though their answers were more nuanced. For example, Carla shared that just because someone is 'Filipino' does not necessarily mean that they can relate to newcomer Filipina/o/x youth but that representation matters:

> To me, it doesn't matter where you're born. In just matters…how committed are you to learning about these students? And we all come with our own biases and our own social location, but if you can think you can fix a classroom by just playing basketball after school, that's a major problem for me. I have yet to meet a social worker that could speak Tagalog at all in schools, and the only Filipino teachers I've met who could speak Tagalog were mechanics.
>
> (Carla)

Particular performances of 'Filipino' tropes such as 'playing basketball', as Carla stated, does not necessarily mean that the social and educational needs of Filipina/o/x youth are being met. Carla implies that educators need to be aware of their biases and social location, which will have an impact on how they relate to newly reunified Filipina/o/x youth. Connection with the students seems to be the most important aspect when it comes to Filipina/o/x educators, according to Carla.

Contesting reductionist representations of 'Filipinos' requires the mobilization of the political agency of Filipina/o/x youth, facilitated by school-community partnerships consisting of Filipina/o/x community leaders. While Filipina/o/x youth had various perspectives on the representation of Filipina/o/x teachers in educational systems, I draw on Hall's (1997) "through the eye of representation", a counter-strategy to contest reductionist stereotypes where the main concern is, "with the *forms* of racial representation than with introducing new *content*. It accepts and works with the shifting, unstable character of meaning, and enters, as it were, into a struggle over representation, while acknowledging that, since meaning can never be finally fixed, there can never be any real victories." (emphasis in original) (p. 274). The meaning of identity constantly shifts rather than remaining the same and 'essentialist', particularly with the various intergenerational and intersectional identities and social locations that the Filipina/o/x community belong to. I posit that these educational factors within school-community partnerships are significant as they impact how Filipina/o/x youth understand their transnational identities in relation to settler colonialism, decolonization, and Indigenous Nations in Canada.

To address these concerns, Darlene, a community leader, stated that having Filipina/o/x teachers represented in school systems may also help to create "opportunities for us to create a dialogue and [bridge] differences." Curious, I asked, "So that could also apply to teachers who are not Filipino then, too?" to which Darlene replied, "Yeah, definitely, teachers need constant evaluations from the people that they are teaching, yes, otherwise, [teaching] become[s] disconnected." Similar to Carla's perspective, connecting with Filipina/o/x students seems to be the salient factor when it comes to their social and economic well-being. Thus, the representation of Filipina/o/x educators in the school system is important in order to challenge, "reductionist notions of racial and gender affiliation…[and to] make available an alternative social imaginary…beyond heteronormative constraints and the persistence of colonialism" (Martino & Rezai-Rashti, 2012, p. 243). To address the concerns of "just playing basketball", as Carla mentioned above, which is a "reductionist racial affiliation" (Martino & Rezai-Rashti, 2012, p. 243), it is important to evaluate what is most important to the students, as Darlene stated above. Martino & Rezai-Rashti (2012) argue that students provided:

> Explicit details and information about what they consider to really matter in their assessment of their teachers. They highlight pedagogical dimensions related to teachers' capacity or willingness to (i) relate and provide a supportive classroom environment; (ii) allow for flexibility in the delivery of the curriculum; (iii) treat students fairly and with respect; (iv) connect the curriculum to student interests and everyday lives; (v) provide extra support and to scaffold learning; (vi) build pedagogical relationship with students that resonate with their idea of the meaning of friendship; (vii) explain difficult concepts and content; (viii) make learning fun; and (ix) avoid expressing anger and the tendency to yell or shout.
>
> (p. 237)

Connecting the curriculum to Filipina/o/x youth and their lived experience exhibits transnational feminist (Nagar & Swarr, 2010) & critical emotional (Zembylas, 2012) praxes that would the facilitate the political agency of Filipina/o/x youth and the deepened understandings of their intersectional and transnational identities in relation to Indigenous Nations. Many of the youth resonated with Martino and Rezai-Rashti's (2012) findings that they needed the teachers to be supportive and to treat them with respect. In Kelly's (2014) findings, "the lack of role models in the larger community, especially for young boys, is a related problem. Representations and racialization of Filipino identity within wider Canadian society, and the nonrecognition of that identity in school curricula, also play a role (p. 1). In my study, Filipina/o/x youth and their mothers had various perspectives on this, and disagreed and agreed about the importance of having Filipina/o/x role models as teachers. Given that the answers were varied and nuanced surrounding the concern of Filipina/o/x role models in the school system demonstrates the "complexities and ambivalences of representation itself" (Hall, 1996, p. 274). In his last point, Hall (1996) talked about the *politics of representation*, that "the body [is] the principal site of its representational strategies [as it has been] caught up in the complexities of power and subordination within representation" (p. 274).

Furthering the argument of collaboration and Indigenous-migrant-settler relations, a Filipina community leader in the educational system, Sherry, shared that Filipina/o/x leaders and students alike were going through their own identity and belonging processes. Sherry possesses a thorough understanding of anti-oppressive and decolonization processes, particularly around Indigenous-settler relations. As a second-generation Filipina-Canadian, she positions herself in relation to newcomer Filipina/o/x youth as we, myself included, have multiple transnational identities:

> To acknowledge that...we are still learning more about ourselves in this context and by learning with them and feeling some of the things that they're doing, we then get to learn deeper about ourselves, so for the young people that come here, you know, for the students, it's good that more of these opportunities to learn with other cultures is happening, but how do we facilitate? What do they understand about identity in this context, right, coming to Canada as an immigrant, and how do we support developing that identity for them because that's a hard one, and that goes again to that piece of being reflected in who is your support system, in your communities, and in your education system, because you are still developing an identity, you don't have people to reflect back to you something strong and positive. And how are you supposed to feel about yourself? How are you supposed to know you can move forward and achieve things when that's not being reflected to you? So, I think that plays hand in hand.
>
> (Sherry)

Sherry engages in questions of Filipina/o/x representation among community leaders within the educational system as well as the intersectional and transnational identities of Filipina/o/x students, particularly in how the construction of identities play out intergenerationally. She draws attention to the role that educational systems, community leaders, and social services play in Filipina/o/x youth's transnational identities and highlighted how Filipina/o/x community leaders may help facilitate the youths' agency through representation. The reflexivity of community leaders are an important piece of this process, particularly with regard to Nagar and Swarr's (2010) conceptualization of transnational feminist praxis, where "collaboration [is] as an intellectual and political tool…that [interweaves] theories and practices of knowledge production through collaborative dialogues [which] provides a way to radically rethink existing approaches to subalternity, voice, authorship, and representation" (p. 2). This implies that making of the transnational and intersectional identities of Filipina/o/x youth and school-community partnerships, including Filipina/o/x community leaders, is a collaborative process where the political agency of Filipina/o/x youth plays a significant role.

Role of Community Involvement and advocacy

When I had asked Filipina/o/x youth about their school experiences, they expressed having benefitted from these services and partnerships on a significant level. However, there are still incidents of discrimination and racism that these systems can learn from in order to ensure that transnational students' social and educational needs have been met. In linking the school experiences of recently reunified youth through the L/CP, Caro (2009) stated that in terms of community involvement, this specific group of newcomer youth greatly benefitted from connecting with community activist organizations, "their lives significantly changed as a result of their being involved in [a] Filipino community organization…if schools cannot provide education and support in terms of immigrant youth understanding their situations better, community organizations should be given more support in order to provide educational discussions and workshops which allow the youth to understand their situations" (p. 87). Therefore, school-community partnerships are key to meet the social and economic needs of Filipina/o/x youth in understanding their migration experiences through the L/CP, particularly the gendered vulnerabilities of their mothers (Jaggar, 2009) in relation to Indigenous Nations. Filipina/o/x youth demonstrate that their agency is relationally-constituted (Hörschelmann & El Refaie, 2014) upon school-community partnerships. What helped Angelica feel supported was having access to the school settlement workers during lunch hour and after-school, "Settlement workers, they're the best!… they're the ones who like [to] give me the opportunities to have the information [and] the resources" (Angelica). Natalia, Angelica's mother, also pointed out how helpful the school settlement workers had been for Angelica and her brother, Brandon: "I must say that ever since they came to Canada, they have changed for the better. They became more hardworking, confident, and athletic, unlike when they were in the Philippines...Back then, they were too shy when it comes to presenting [them]selves. Now, both of them [have] a passion for leadership, which is why I am thankful for the settlement workers who helped my kids. They were the ones who brought out the best in my kids" (Natalia). School-community partnerships are an excellent step towards meeting the educational and social needs of transnational students. Addressing the culturally-specific needs of Filipina/o/x students helps to situate the experiences of transnational youth who come through the L/CP as, "situated knowledges are about communities, not about isolated individuals. The only way to find a larger vision is to be somewhere in particular" (Haraway, 1988, p. 590). Angelica suggested the following for improving the school experiences of transnational students:

Researcher: So what do you wish to see...to have a better school experience?

Angelica: Maybe more programs for newcomers cause people need to be more open-minded that it's not easy for newcomers to adjust and it's kind of tough if everyone else sees themselves as superior to others because they've been here a while.

Researcher: So maybe some education for not [only] the newcomers but for the ones who have been here, like the Canadian students, like understanding for, and welcoming of, newcomers, right? So that's what you would like to see more? Not necessarily from the teachers but from your peers?

Angelica: Yeah

Angelica's suggestion for improving the school experiences for transnational students may be beneficial for all students, not just those who have recently arrived. Her observation of others who see themselves as 'superior' connects with Fanon's (1986) argument that colonialism created hierarchies:

> However painful it may be for me to accept this conclusion, I am obliged to state it: For the black man there is only one destiny. And it is white. Before beginning the case, I have to say certain things. The analysis that I am undertaking is psychological. In spite of this it is apparent to me that the effective disalienation of the black man entails an immediate recognition of social and economic realities. If there is an inferiority complex, it is the outcome of a double process:...primarily, economic... subsequently, the internalization...or, better, the epidermalization...of this inferiority.
>
> (pp. 12–13)

Angelica's suggestion speaks to the role transnational feminist praxis plays within school-community partnerships: through a strategic and deliberate collaboration among institutions and community members can reclaim marginal spaces (Nagar & Swarr, 2010). Community agencies, such as the SDC, seem to achieve this 'strategic and deliberate' (Nagar & Swarr, 2010) collaboration among institutions through its location at the school, making services for students accessible. The NSC also made after-school programs accessible to students by travelling to the schools, though having the site on school property could potentially increase accessibility for students. Nevertheless, both the SDC and the NSC epitomized an ethic of care, relationality, and support for Filipina/o/x youth as they attempted to address their social and educational needs.

Conclusion

In this chapter I addressed the role of school-community partnerships, specifically in their educational role in dismantling settler-colonialism through decolonization in relation to Indigenous Nations. Moreover, I also examine how despite the capacity for school-community partnerships and education to reproduce colonial power relations, such partnerships have also made moves towards facilitating Filipina/o/x youths' understanding of their intersectional identities in relation to Indigenous Nations. Indeed, my research revealed that school-community partnerships provided space for youth to learn about residential schooling and the need to connect with Indigenous communities as a decolonial pedagogical praxis. Filipina/o/x community leaders, youth, and mothers provide their perspectives on Filipina/o/x educators and while some aspects of colonializations have influenced these perspectives, there is also space to resist through transnational feminist and critical emotional praxes. Overall, this chapter illuminated the role of school-community partnerships in facilitating the making of critical social justice action through migrant-Indigenous and racial solidarities and how these solidarities are situated yet are contingent and relational.

References

Amadahy, Z., & Lawrence, B. (2009). Indigenous peoples and Black people in Canada: Settlers or allies? In A. Kempf (Ed.), *Breaching the Colonial Contract: Anti-Colonialism in the US and Canada* (pp. 105–136). New York: Springer.

Anthias, F. (2011). Intersections and translocations: New paradigms for thinking about cultural diversity and social identities. *European Educational Research Journal, 10*(2), 204–217.

Bauder, H., & Breen, R. (2022). Indigenous perspectives of immigration policy in a settler country. *Journal of International Migration and Integration, 24(*1), 369–384. https://doi.org/10.1007/s12134-022-00951-4

Caro, J. F. (2009). The educational experiences of Filipino youth in Quebec in the context of global migration. ProQuest Dissertations & Theses.

Constantino, R. (1996). The Miseducation of the Filipino. Retrieved from: https://www.scribd.com/doc/32721186/Renato-Constantino-The-Miseducation-of-the-Filipino.

Constantino, R. (1996). *The Miseducation of the Filipino*. Retrieved from: https://www.scribd.com/doc/32721186/Renato-Constantino-The-Miseducation-of-the-Filipino

Curley, A., Gupta, P., Lookabaugh, L., Neubert, C., & Smith, S. (2022). Decolonisation is a political Project: Overcoming Impasses between Indigenous Sovereignty and Abolition. *Antipode*, *54(*4), 1043–1062. https://doi.org/10.1111/anti.12830

Espiritu, Y.L. (2003). Filipino American lives across cultures, communities, and countries (Adobe Digital Editions). Retrieved from: http://ebookcentral.proquest.com.ezproxy.library.yorku.ca/lib/york/detail.action?docID=224026.

Fanon, F. (1986). *Black skin, White masks* (C.L. Markmann, Trans.). London: Pluto Press. (Original work published 1952).

Farrales, M. (2019). Repurposing beauty pageants: The colonial geographies of Filipina pageants in Canada. *Environment and Planning. D, Society & Space*, *37*(1), 46–64. https://doi.org/10.1177/0263775818796502

Hall, S. (1996). *Questions of Cultural Identity*. SAGE. https://web-p-ebscohost-com.library.smu.ca/ehost/detail/detail?vid=0&sid=c6cc466d-3d7b-4678-ab0e-c7ac0e06a92a%40redis&bdata=JnNpdGU9ZWhvc3QtbGl2ZQ%3d%3d#AN=716879&db=e000xna

Hall, S. (1997). *Representation: Cultural Representations and Signifying Practices*. London: SAGE.

Haraway, D. (1988). Situated knowledges: The science question in feminism and the privilege of partial perspective. *Feminist Perspectives*, *14*(3), 575–599.

Hörschelmann, K., & El Refaie, E. (2014). Transnational citizenship, dissent and the political geographies of youth. *Transactions*

Jaggar, A.M (2009). Transnational cycles of gendered vulnerability: A prologue to the Theory of global gender justice. *Philosophical Topics*, 33–52.

Kelly, P. (2014). *Understanding Intergenerational Social Mobility: Filipino Youth in Canada*. IRPP Study 45. Montreal: Institute for Research On Public Policy.

Lawrence, B. & Dua, E. (2005). Decolonizing anti-racism. *Social Justice 32*(4), 120–143.

Mahtani, M & Roberts, D. (2012). Contemplating new spaces in Canadian studies. In R.S. Coloma., B. McElhinny, E. Tungohan, J.P.C. Cantugal & L.M Davidson (Eds.), *Filipinos in Canada: Disturbing Invisibility* (pp. 417–426). Toronto, ON: University of Toronto.

Martino, W., & Rezai-Rashti, G. (2012). *Gender, Race and the Politics of Role Modeling: The Influence of Male Teachers*. New York: Routledge.

Mohanty, C.T. (2003). *Feminism without Borders: Decolonizing Theory, Practicing Solidarity*. Durham, NC: Duke University Press.

Nagar, R., & Swarr, A. L. (2010). *Critical Transnational Feminist Praxis*. Albany: SUNY Press.https://library.smu.ca/login?url=https://search.ebscohost.com/login.aspx?direct=true&db=e000xna&AN=306680&site=ehost-live

Pierce, L.M. (2005). Not just my closet: Exposing familial, cultural, and imperial skeletons. In M.L de Jesús, (Ed.), *Pinay Power: Peminist Critical Theory: Theorizing the Filipina/American Experience*, (pp. 31–44). New York: Routledge.

Pratt, G. (2012). *Families Apart: Migrant Mothers and Conflicts of Labour and Love*. Minneapolis, MN: University of Minnesota Press.

Ticar, J. E. (2017). *Investigating the Transnational Identities of Filipina/o/x Youth in Toronto Urban High Schools: A Critical Ethnographic Study of the Impact of Canada's Live-In/Caregiver Program*. ProQuest Dissertations & Theses.

Tuck, E. (2009). Suspending damage: A letter to communities. *Harvard Educational Review 79*(3), 409–428.

Tuck, E., & Yang, K. W. (2012). Decolonization is not a metaphor. *Decolonization: Indigeneity, Education & Society, 1*(1), 1–40. https://jps.library.utoronto.ca/index.php/des/article/view/18630/15554

Tungohan, E. (2012). Debunking notions of migrant 'Victimhood': A critical assessment of temporary labour migration programs and Filipina migrant activism in Canada. In R.S. Coloma., B. McElhinny, E. Tungohan, J.P.C. Catungal & L.M Davidson (Eds.), *Filipinos in Canada: Disturbing Invisibility* (pp. 161–80), Toronto, ON: University of Toronto.

Yuval-Davis, N. (2006). Belonging and the politics of belonging. *Patterns of Prejudice, 40*(3), 197–214.

Yuval-Davis, N. (2011). *The Politics of Belonging: Intersectional Contestations*. London: SAGE.

Zembylas, M. (2012). Transnationalism, migration and emotions: Implications for education. *Globalisation, Societies and Education, 10*(2), 163–179.

7 Conclusion

In this book, I wanted to showcase the ways in which Filipina mothers and their children mobilize their political agency in relation to school-community partnerships, which mainly consisted of Filipina/o/x community leaders from two social service agencies, the Newcomer Support Centre (NSC) and Services for a Diverse Community (SDC) in Toronto urban schools. The book offers a gendered, critical analysis of policies and practices that give rise to a specific experience of trauma due to systemic oppression and the legacy of colonization, with the explicit purpose of highlighting the *embodied* ways in which Filipina/o/x youth manifest their *political agency* and achieve a sense of identity and belonging, alongside advocacy, community, and systemic support. Moreover, it looks at how Filipina mothers mobilize their gendered vulnerabilities (Jaggar, 2009) through their navigation of Canada's Live-in/Caregiver Program (L/CP) through relational intersectionality, where there is space for empowerment and resistance within forms of oppression (Collins, 2000; 2019). The book also illuminated the engagement of school-community partnerships in transnational feminist praxis (Nagar & Swarr, 2010) to facilitate Filipina/o/x youths' political agency as they navigate the traumas of family separation and reunification through the L/CP, as racialized, gendered, sexual and faith/spiritual subjects. The impact of such partnerships was also highlighted in drawing attention to the role of settlement workers in educating the youth about the underlying reasons their mothers had left them behind, as well as how to engage in critical social justice through solidarity and allyships with marginalized groups, specifically with Indigenous and other racialized communities. Ultimately the significance of this book lies in its the youths' deep insights that transform the 'fragments' of their narratives (Pratt, 2010) into advocacy sites, in relation to their mothers, their peers, and community leaders' perspectives, leading to recommendations in educational and im/migration policies and practices, particularly through decolonization and critical social justice.

Advocacy implications

The youth in the book reported many emotions when reflecting on their experiences of family separation and reunification, highlighting that it is the youth's affective and embodied experiences of transnational migration that need to

DOI: 10.4324/9781003287469-7

be the driving force of policy and pedagogical change in educational systems (Zembylas, 2012). For policy makers, educational systems, and social services to understand the impact of family separation and reunification on the youth, I drew on Zembylas (2012) who recommended that educators and educational policies pay attention to emotion that is at the heart of the dynamics between micro and macro level dimensions of local realities as it speaks to who gets included/excluded in the classroom:

> [An] investigation of emotions that is grounded in the transactions between macro- political aspects and the micro-politics of local realities. Therefore, exploring the connections between certain emotions about migrants in society and educational institutions, on the one hand, and hegemonic social structures and power relations, on the other, allows us to better understand the formation of emotional economies in educational institutions, their effects and the openings to subvert them. Examining which educational policies and practices generate particular emotional economies and emotion norms constitutes another interesting area of investigation.
>
> (p. 175)

The embodied emotions of the Filipina/o/x youth and their mothers mobilize are advocacy sites that are subversive in that they challenge the power relations embedded within the L/CP. School-community partnerships, as collaborators, highlighted the need for educational policies and practices to address income supports for economically disadvantaged families:

> The more highly resourced the family, the better the educational environment typically available to children, and the stronger their educational achievement. A policy of income supports for poor families could, in this sense, be understood as a crucial educational policy. If educators were to include in the panoply of policies they promote a set of strategies to provide income supports for poor and low-income families, and if such policies were passed and implemented in our cities, urban students could be provided with more highly resourced early learning environments.
>
> (Anyon, 2013, p. 376)

Moreover, this book revealed that social services need the financial support to sustain programs and partnerships that are beneficial for the youth and their families, with community leaders serving to build access points to engage in solidarities with Indigenous Nations and marginalized groups through decolonization. For policy makers, it is important to become aware of the delays and barriers that occur prior to family reunification due to large amount of paperwork and administration fees, which community leaders had consistently reiterated in the interviews. Many migrant advocacy groups have recommended permanent residency upon arrival so as to avoid prolonged family separation and reunification and policy protection for migrant workers. Migrant workers themselves are part of organizations and advocate for the rights of other migrant workers in the Temporary Foreign Workers Program, a program the L/CP is a part of:

> [Migrant work] is an opportunity to get employment, it's an opportunity to support your family, but the conditions are really difficult and you have to be strong-willed to survive it…Status upon arrival is [the] only demand we have. It's the only remedy that will bring about equality and fairness to these workers.
>
> (CBC/Radio-Canada, 2016)

Status upon arrival would also minimize the precarity transnational Filipina/o/x families face through the L/CP. Throughout this book, Filipina/o/x youth expressed hurt, anger, and strained relationships as their mothers usually work long hours in precarious low-wage jobs. Additionally, some of these parents are single-mothers working multiple jobs. Thus, partnerships are recommended to improve migration policy:

> Exploring alliances with other groups also become crucial. After all, the evolution of migrant care worker policy in Canada shows that…organizations need to be persistent as well as creative in their responses to state abuse. The formation of partnerships at this stage may create the impetus to create stronger measures against migrant worker abuse and to provide live-in caregivers and other migrant workers access to citizenship.
>
> (Tungohan, 2012, p. 177)

For social services and educators, further professional support and development of programs and training around the specific experiences of youth who experienced family separation and reunification would be beneficial for transnational families. Community consultation with the Filipina/o/x families as well as other transnational communities may help to facilitate this process as their voices need to be central to the collaborative projects within these partnerships. This knowledge needs to be continually disseminated to policy makers, social services, and educational policies. For policy makers at the government level, recommendations for funding would assist in sustaining such vital collaborative programs for transnational youth and their families.

Methodologically, my book also revealed the utility of employing other means for data collection to supplement or use as an alternative to traditional methods to verbal interviews, particularly with participants whose experiences may be difficult to talk about, such as the youth who have experienced family separation and reunification through the L/CP (see Pratt, 2010). In this respect,

I recommend critical arts-based inquiry, particularly given its capacity to allow more for subjects to express the affective dimensions of their embodied experiences of belonging and to create spaces for the researcher to explore such aspects of experience through visual representation made available through art forms (Finley, 2011).

Another important aspect that requires some further investigation has to do with the need to explore the question of religion and spirituality in its capacity to generate further insights into how religion/spirituality and agency intersect and impact transnational students such as Filipina/o/x youth in terms of how they make sense of their own identity and belonging in urban schools such as in Toronto. As part of her identity and belonging process, Anzaldúa (1999) engaged in the impact of colonialism on her identity through her spirituality and through the concept of borderlands, "the Third World grates against the first and bleeds…[and] the lifeblood of two worlds merge to form a third country – a border culture" (Anzaldúa, 1999, p. 25). These particular concepts of borderlands, the sacred, and spiritual (Dillard & Okpalaoka, 2011) are important aspects of migration and educational research because the youth signified the importance of their religious/spiritual identities within their global migration experiences. The intersection between religion/spirituality and sexuality would facilitate deeper understandings of political agency, which is contingent upon the policies of the L/CP, and strengthen the praxes of school-community partnerships in Toronto urban schools.

References

Anyon, J. A. (2013). Political economy of race, urban education, and educational policy. In C. McCarthy, W. Crichlow, G. Dimitriadis, & N. Dolby (Eds.), *Race, identity, and representation in education* (2nd ed.) (pp. 369–378). Routledge Taylor & Francis Group.

Anzaldúa, G. (1999). *Borderlands/La frontera* (2nd ed.). Aunt Lute Books.

CBC/Radio-Canada. (2016). Migrant workers need permanent residency status, labour advocates say: Justice for migrant workers launches Ontario-wide tour. http://www.cbc.ca/news/canada/windsor/permanent-residency-migrant-workers-1.3748911

Collins, P. H. (2019). Relationality within intersectionality. In *Intersectionality as critical social theory* (pp. 225–252). Duke University Press. https://doi.org/10.1515/9781478007098-009

Collins, P. H. (2000). *Black feminist thought: Knowledge, consciousness, and the politics of empowerment*. Routledge. https://doi.org/10.4324/978020390005

Dillard, C. B., & Okpalaoka, C. (2011). The sacred and spiritual nature of endarkened transnational feminist praxis in qualitative research. In N. K. Denzin, & Y. S. Lincoln (Eds.), *SAGE handbook of qualitative research* (pp. 147–162). SAGE.

Finley, S. (2011). Critical arts-based inquiry: The pedagogy and performance of a radical ethical aesthetic. In N. Denzin, & Y. Lincoln (Eds.), *The SAGE handbook of qualitative research* (pp. 435–450). SAGE.

Jaggar, A. M. (2009). Transnational cycles of gendered vulnerability: A prologue to the theory of global gender justice. *Philosophical Topics*, 33–52.

Nagar, R., & Swarr, A. L. (2010). *Critical transnational feminist praxis*. State University of New York Press.
Pratt, G. (2010). Listening for spaces of ordinariness: Filipino-Canadian youths' transnational lives. *Children's Geographies*, *8*(4), 343–352.
Tungohan, E. (2012). Debunking notions of migrant 'Victimhood': A critical assessment of temporary labour migration programs and Filipina migrant activism in Canada. In R. S. Coloma, B. McElhinny, E. Tungohan, J. P. C. Catungal, & L. M. Davidson (Eds.), *Filipinos in Canada: Disturbing invisibility* (pp. 161–80). University of Toronto.
Zembylas, M. (2012). Transnationalism, migration and emotions: Implications for education. *Globalisation, Societies and Education*, *10*(2), 163–179.

Appendix A

Interview Questions for Doctoral Dissertation

Appendix 1: Youth interview questions

Green Zone:

1 What was your understanding of why your parent/guardian(s) had to work in Toronto?
2 What was your experience like when you first moved to Toronto from the Philippines?
3 When you were in the Philippines, how did you imagine Toronto to be like?
4 How did you remain in contact with your parent/guardian(s) when they were in Canada and you were in the Philippines? How was it like to see them again when you first reunited?

Yellow Zone:

5 What kinds of cultural traditions did/do you value? What are the important events that you attend(ed), if any?
6 If you identify as an Indigenous person, describe some of your traditions, experiences, and practices
7 If you identify with a religious and/or spiritual belief, what are your practices and how are they important to you?
8 How do your parent(s)/guardian(s), friends, and other people you know, expect males and females to behave and act? What do you think about these beliefs and practices?
9 What are your ideas about how skin colour matters to Filipina/o/xs both in the Philippines and in Toronto? How have you been affected by these ideas?
10 If you identify as a non-heterosexual or 'queer' or some other definition that you use to describe your sexuality, what was your experience like growing up? What is your experience like here in Toronto?
11 What was it like for you and your family once you moved to Toronto? How was it different from your life in Toronto? Was it difficult economically for the family?

Blue Zone:

12 What are some of your important and special memories of people, places, events, things, etc., before leaving the Philippines and first moving to Canada? What are some memorabilia that you have taken with you to Toronto, and/or what do you do to keep connected to the memories, people, places, events, etc. in the Philippines?
13 What were your school experiences like in the Philippines? What was your experience of adjusting to your school in Toronto?
14 How were your teachers and classmates helpful during the adjustment to a new school in Toronto? What did you appreciate and what did you wish to see so that you could have had a better educational experience?
15 What was your idea of an excellent teacher in the Philippines? Have your teachers in Toronto demonstrated any of these qualities?
16 What are your thoughts of having a Filipina/o/x teacher as a role model in Toronto?
17 What are your thoughts about how people of different racial backgrounds and Indigenous peoples and tribes are treated in your schools, both in Toronto and in the Philippines, and in the wider communities, both in Toronto and in the Philippines?

Appendix 2: Parent interview questions

1 What were your main reasons for moving to Toronto as a caregiver?
2 What are your hopes, expectations, and dreams for your child's success?
3 What is your experience like with your child's school? How is your relationship like with the educators and administrators?
4 What are some of the things that you like about your child's school?
5 What are some of the things that you would like your child's school to improve on?
6 Do you think it would make a difference if your child's teacher is Filipina/o/x? If so, how will this help your child? If not, why?
7 In your opinion, has your child been successful in school?
8 How has your child's school been helpful in his/her adjustment to Canada?

Appendix 3: Community leader interview questions

1 What are the main concerns that you see among Filipina/o/x youth and their parents/guardians/mothers?
2 How would you describe the school success rate among Filipina/o/x youth in your programmes?
3 From your experience, how have schools been helpful in Filipina/o/x youths' adjustment to Toronto?
4 What are some of the improvements you would like to see in educational system?

5 What are some of the concerns that parents/guardians/mothers and Filipina/o/x youth have discussed about school?
6 Do you think that it would benefit Filipina/o/x youth to have more Filipina/o/x teachers as role models? Why? If so, how do you think that this will improve student success rates?
7 How do your programmes help Filipina/o/x students adjust to Toronto and to their school?

Appendix B
Interview Questions for Postdoctoral Research

Semi-structured interview questions for social service providers

1 What is your understanding of anti-racism and/or anti-oppressive practice?
2 What are your equity, diversity, and inclusion policies and how do you implement these?
3 In your services and/or interventions, (without breaking confidentiality) what are the main issues that you see among Filipina/o/x families who have been reunified through Canada's Live-in/Caregiver Program (L/CP)?
4 What are the strengths that the Filipina/o/x families who have experienced reunification through L/CP possess?
5 How does the Filipina/o/x community understand their experiences of family separation and reunification? How do they transform these experiences as a form of empowerment (general experiences, no need to break client/recipient confidentiality)?
6 What types of interventions and/or services do you employ when working with Filipina/o/x families who have experienced family separation and reunification through the L/CP?

Semi-structured interview questions for Filipina/o/x families (through verbal and/or creative expression)

Session 1: Separation Period

1 For the youth: what was your experience like when you were separated from your mother/parent?
2 For the former caregiver parent: what was your experience like when you were separated from your children and family?
3 For other family member(s): what was your experience like when you were separated from the former caregiver?
4 For the youth: How was it like to hear the experiences of the former caregiver and other family member(s)?
5 For the former caregiver and family member(s): How was it like to hear the experiences of the youth?

Session 2: During Reunification

What are some of the memories that you have of family reunification?

1 What were some of the experiences you faced during family reunification? If there were any concerns, how did you overcome them?
2 What were your experiences like when you accessed social services? What did you appreciate, what would you like to see more of (improvement?)
3 How did you learn and grow together as a family who recently reunified?
4 What did you learn about yourselves as individuals? As a family?

Session 3: After Reunification

1 What are your hopes and dreams for the future as a family and as individuals?
2 What are your recommendations for the services that you received?
3 Upon reflection, what has helped you adjust to your new family dynamics?
4 How do you continue to build your relationship as a family?
5 How do you continue to learn more about your individual and collective identities as a reunified Filipina/o/x family (in relation to other community members who have had similar experiences?)

Index

Italicized and **bold** pages refer to figures and tables respectively, and page numbers followed by "n" refer to notes

For Product Safety Concerns and Information please contact our EU
representative GPSR@taylorandfrancis.com
Taylor & Francis Verlag GmbH, Kaufingerstraße 24, 80331 München, Germany

www.ingramcontent.com/pod-product-compliance
Lightning Source LLC
LaVergne TN
LVHW010835120826
845149LV00016B/2558

* 9 7 8 1 0 3 2 2 6 2 7 1 0 *